Everyone loves a winner.

But what about those of us—most of us—who do more losing in life than winning? Is there anything worthwhile about coming in second, tenth, or not at all?

Jim Hunter's goal was to be a winner, the world's greatest downhill racer. As a Christian, he was convinced God wanted him number one. With fan support like that, how could he go wrong?

When he won a bronze medal at the 1972 Olympics, eighteen-year-old Jungle Jim was the kid with great potential, possibly the next Jean-Claude Killy. He was brash, arrogant, and aggressive.

But when he didn't win the way he was expected to, Jim learned something about himself, and about God.

This is the story of Jim Hunter and his discovery that there is more than one mountain worth climbing.

JIM HUNTER
A Man Against the Mountain

As told to
MARSHALL SHELLEY

David C. Cook Publishing Co.
ELGIN, ILLINOIS—WESTON, ONTARIO

Edited by Dean Merrill
Designed by Kurt Dietsch
Printed in the United States of America

LC 78-59283
ISBN 0-89191-143-X

To mom, dad, and brother Lorne,
without whose sacrifices,
encouragement, and discipline
I could never have become the skier
God has allowed me to become.

Contents

One
MORZINE

ABOVE TIMBERLINE IN THE ALPS, the January wind has an icy bite, but the view is spectacular. From the top of the downhill run at Morzine, France, you can look into Switzerland on the east, and toward the south, Mont Blanc dominates the French-Italian border.

You're surrounded by mountain peaks, evergreens, and snow-covered slopes. Far below lies the old village of Morzine four miles away. From there, a tramway stretches part of the way up and across the mountain to the modern resort of Avoriaz. The futuristic shapes of the condominiums in Avoriaz seem slightly out of place next to the massive timelessness of the mountains and the quaint chalets of Morzine.

This particular day was overcast and cold—in other words, about normal for a European ski race in January. But the clouds were so low that none of

A MAN AGAINST THE MOUNTAIN

After this giant slalom at Val d'Isere, the retired Jean-Claude Killy was asked if he saw another Killy on the horizon. He named this skier—Jim Hunter.

the scenery was visible—everything was lost in a gray mist.

It didn't matter. I wasn't thinking about the view. I was in Morzine for the sixth World Cup race of the 1973-74 season. In two days would be the downhill event—ninety-six racers from twenty-one countries trying to win World Cup points by hurtling down two miles of mountain faster than anyone else.

Someone once described downhill racers as "kamikaze pilots without wings." It's not much of an exaggeration. Yet the feeling of screaming down a mountain at seventy miles an hour, sometimes reaching ninety, is a sensation I thrive on.

But today I was a little nervous. The season wasn't going that well for me. I had placed fourth in the giant slalom a month before at Val d'Isere, France, in the first race of the year. And just before Christmas, I'd taken a fourth in the downhill at Schladming, Austria. But after four years in Europe with the Canadian national team, I still hadn't placed first in a World Cup race. My desire to win was entering the obsession stage.

Wearing my helmet and skin-tight racing suit, I skied across the mountain from the lift to the starting gate and got ready for a practice run. I glanced down one more time at my Rossignol racing skis. Most racers train on a different pair of skis from the ones they race on. Training skis may have a scratch or some other minute flaw that makes them just a bit slower. Even though other racers bring out their best skis only on race day, I had made a habit of taking my first training run on my best pair and running as hard as I could so I'd be able to see exactly how the course felt under actual racing conditions. I figured there was little danger of damaging my good pair on the first practice run.

This was something I'd picked up from one of my early heroes, Buddy Werner, the American skier who was killed in an avalanche in 1965. I tried to train as Buddy did—full speed all the time, and as many runs as possible.

Yesterday, the Canadian team had inspected the course. We had slowly skied down the slope, noting the different turns, and discussing the fastest route to the bottom. I felt I was familiar with the mountain. I was ready to attack it flat out.

Just before I stepped into the army tent that

served as the starting gate, the binding manufacturer's representative took a quick look at my bindings and said they were okay. I nodded. Then it was time to go.

As I moved into the tent, another racer was just taking off out the other opening on the side. My turn was next, so I positioned myself at the start.

Racers leave every thirty seconds, and when the racer in front of you departs, the longest—and loneliest—half minute of racing begins. I poised myself at the gate, adjusted my helmet and goggles, and crouched ready to spring. Alone with my thoughts, I looked down the course, but because of the low clouds, I could barely see past the first turn. My stomach was tense. Even though I'd been racing for eight years, I still felt the tension. No one can be sure what's going to happen on skis at sixty-plus miles an hour.

Then the starter counted down—*cinq-quatre-trois-deux-un*—and I leaped through the gate, tripping the wand that starts the timer. I shoved off with my poles and skated away on my skis, accelerating as fast as I could.

The first part of the course was soft snow, relatively easy skiing, and I bent into my racing tuck and headed down the steepest route. Pointing straight downhill, I was soon up to about seventy-five miles an hour.

Ahead was a left turn, a hard right, and then a very difficult left. I remembered laughing up at the starting gate at a couple of earlier racers who'd taken a wrong turn here and gotten lost in a field of powder. The markers were a little confusing, but because of our inspection runs, I knew which direction to go. I carved left, then swept right. I came to the timberline, and suddenly trees lined both sides of the course.

As I made the right turn, I shot past Sully Henderson, the Canadian team coach's wife, who was videotaping my run. Then I leaned into the hard left.

This turn was tough for a couple of reasons. First, it was the beginning of the hard snow. On most mountains, the soft snow is at the top of the run, because it's colder up there and the snow doesn't melt. Down below, there's more melting and refreezing. Second, there was a small bump you had to take just before you completed the turn. Most skiers would prejump it—they'd leap into the air ahead of the bump and land on the downward slope. It makes for a smoother landing than flying off the bump itself and smacking your skis on the flats when you finally return to earth. Prejumping requires precise timing, but it's the fastest way to take most bumps. I decided to prejump this one.

But the toughest part about this turn was that you ended it heading across the side of the hill. If you didn't have your turn completed before you hit the sidehill, you'd slide right down the slope into the trees.

I made the turn and prejumped the bump. But when I touched down, suddenly my right ski ejected. A split second later, my left ski also released. I was airborne.

I was still upright, but because of the angle of the turn I had been making, I started to turn in midair, spinning backwards down the hill, toward the trees.

Flying out of control at sixty-five miles an hour doesn't give you much time to think, but I remember saying to myself, "Please let me turn around enough to see the bales. Don't let me hit the back of my head." I had cracked the back of my skull several years before, and the doctors had said if I hit it again, I could be killed.

Just as my head came around, I hit the first row of haybales that lined the course. I was flying high enough that I just caught them with my feet and kept going. I knocked down about thirty feet of snow fence and hit a stack of bales that was set up in front of a tree. My right leg hooked on one side of the bales, my body bounced off, and I wound up back on the edge of the course. Everything was a jumble of snow, hay, trees, arms, and legs.

Suddenly it was over. I was lying face down in the snow, not sure if I was awake, unconscious, or dead.

I opened my eyes and noticed snow all around me. I brushed away what I could, but discovered I couldn't move my legs. I wanted to get up—World Cup racers always try to get right up after a bad fall and ski the rest of the way down. I didn't want anyone to see I was hurt.

Then the pain hit. It was unbearable.

It's funny how certain things flash through your mind at times like that. I remember saying, "God, if you want me to quit, I'll quit." I had always believed that I needed to rely on God in order to ski my best, and in the past few races, I felt I'd been relying too much on myself and forgetting God's contribution. My first thought was *Is God punishing me?*

I pulled off my helmet, goggles, and mask and started yelling:

"Help me get up!"

The strange thought occurred to me that everyone else spoke French, German, or Italian, and I was yelling in English. But I figured they'd get the gist.

I tried to roll over on my back, but the pain was too much. I hurt all over, but the right knee four times as much as the rest. I just closed my eyes and dropped my face in the snow, wishing I could go to sleep.

Finally some course marshals got to me and wrapped me up. They radioed the starter to stop the training runs, but Andy Mill, from the United States, was already on the course. He flashed by, just missing me.

Someone put an airbag on each of my legs, placed me on a toboggan, and brought me down the hill. As I got to the bottom, Hans Peter Rohr, the American coach, leaned over me and said, "Are you going to be all right, Jimmy?"

"I think so."

By this time, the pain had subsided quite a bit. The air bags let me begin to relax. Maybe I'd still be able to race next month in the FIS World Championships in Saint Moritz, Switzerland.

The FIS (Federation Internationale de Ski) World Championships are held every four years, on the even-numbered years between Olympics. I didn't make the team in 1970 because I was too young, but ever since the 1972 Olympics, where I'd won a bronze medal, I'd been looking forward to the 1974 World Championships. Each race of the 1973-74 season meant a little more because of the upcoming event.

As I lay there on the toboggan, I tried to smile at everyone who came over to see me. Many people greeted me in French, German, and Italian. I wasn't sure of their exact words, but I appreciated their concern. I wanted everyone to think I'd still be able to race at Saint Moritz.

When I got to the clinic, the doctors took X rays and gave me the news: torn ligaments in the right knee. I called back to Canada and talked to my dad, who talked to my doctor. They both agreed I should come home, because surgery might be necessary. By this time, my knee was also telling me that this wasn't just a minor twist. I had to admit I wouldn't race in this year's World Championships. It was a huge disappointment.

The next plane to Canada didn't leave for four days, so I got to lie around and do a lot of thinking. What bothered me even more than the injury was the question *Why did the skis come off?*

So when Scott Henderson, coach of the Canadian team, came to my room the next day, I asked him about it.

"Scotty, there's something wrong. Those skis shouldn't have come off. They were my best pair. I raced with them on boilerplate ice at Garmisch just four days ago."

"Didn't you fall first?"

"No," I said emphatically. It's important to a downhill skier to identify what causes a fall. It's a disgrace to fall unless there's some malfunction. An unexcused wipeout is hard to live down.

Scott hadn't seen my spill. He'd just heard over the two-way radio that I'd fallen and been hurt.

Then I remembered something.

"Scotty, didn't Sully have the video machine on the turn above? Let's bring it in here and look at it."

Scott brought in the videotape recorder, and we looked at the replay of my run. Just before I went out of sight around the third turn, we could see my ski darting off to the right—and I was still in my crouch.

"Where are my skis now?"

"Probably in the ski room," Scott replied.

I asked to see them, along with a pair of training skis for comparison. We inspected the bindings, and the springs in the racing skis were softer than those on the training skis. They were apparently meant for recreational bindings, not racing bindings, which have to withstand more pressure.

I still don't know what happened. Perhaps the springs weakened and went undetected, or perhaps someone had put in the wrong type by mistake. What I did know for sure was that my hopes for a world championship were demolished.

Earlier in the season, after the Val d'Isere race, the great Jean-Claude Killy, now retired, had been asked if he saw another Killy on the horizon. He'd said Jim Hunter of Canada. Naturally, I was honored, and I was determined to prove him right.

But now, just a few weeks later, I was making that long flight across the Atlantic, my leg throbbing and my mind confused. Why had it happened? Should I try to ski again? A new mountain had been placed in my way. I wasn't sure if I could scale this one.

At this point in my life, I was still convinced that God wanted me to be a winner. Couldn't I be more of an influence for him if I were recognized as a winner? Fourth place finishes weren't worth much. And what possible use were people who didn't finish in the top ten? Or who couldn't even race because of torn ligaments?

It looked like Jean-Claude was wrong.

Two
A MARKED MAN

WHY DOES ANYONE want to risk life, limb, and tendon chasing a medal and a bit of temporary recognition? As I flew home to face possible surgery and certainly a long, painful rehabilitation, I thought about why I was racing, and I recalled how I first got into serious competition. Ironically, it was because of another fall.

It was the spring of 1963, and I was ten years old. My younger brother, Lorne, and I were jumping on my bed in the basement of our farmhouse in Shaunavon, Saskatchewan. We were trying little half flips and landing on our behinds. It was fun, if not too great for the bed. Then one of us got the bright idea to try a back flip. Naturally, I had to try it first.

Instead of jumping straight up like I should have, though, I jumped backwards. When I came down, the flip was only half done. I landed on the iron bar at the end of the bed, fell to the floor, and cracked the back of my head on the cement. Everything went black.

Lorne told me later that just as I jumped, my older sister, Marilyn, walked into the room. She saw where I was going to land, and she screamed.

Mom came running, carried me to the car, and raced me to the Shaunavon hospital, but I didn't regain consciousness. I was in a coma for three days.

When I was still unconscious after the third day, the doctor had a drug flown in from Saskatoon. He was hesitant to use it, he said, because it was new, and he wasn't absolutely sure of its effects.

Both of my parents knew Dr. Green well. Mom was a receptionist at the Shaunavon Health Clinic (besides milking dairy cattle every morning at six and every afternoon at five, and also serving as a Sunday school superintendent). Over the years, she had told Dr. Green of her trust in God, and the two of them had discussed their views of faith several times. Now mom told him about all the people who were praying for me—people from Shaunavon Alliance Church, where we attended, people from camps and small churches in the area where my dad had directed choirs.

Mom and dad were praying, too. I learned later that they had told God they wouldn't hold on to me. They recognized my life was in his hands, and they were trusting God to work the situation out either way—whether I lived or died. They assured

Dr. Green that they believed God was still in control and encouraged him to try whatever he felt he had to do.

Finally Dr. Green injected the drug, and everyone waited.

About three hours later, I woke up.

It was a strange world I awakened to. I didn't know where I was. Being in a cold, tall room where I'd never been before was scary. Looking at the bare walls, I tried to remember who I was and why I was there. I couldn't.

My memory was gone. I didn't even know my own name. All I could remember was that my parents were Lloyd and Peggy Hunter, that we were Christians, and that I wanted to be a missionary someday. That was all.

Slowly, after visits from my family and friends, my memory gradually returned. Eventually my head healed, although I'll always be able to feel the crack along the back of my skull. The doctors said if I hit the back of my head again, it could kill me.

After several weeks, I was able to leave the hospital. The cracked cranium had a lingering effect, though—one that indirectly led me to the sport that would take me to Morzine. The concussion permanently affected my ability to remember and my ability to concentrate.

Up until that time, I loved to compete for grades. In grade three, for instance, I had mostly O's (for outstanding) and A's, with a few B's. Shirley Lamoth, my cousin Lorraine Billington, and I were always fighting it out for the best marks in school.

The next year, the teachers chose the three of us to be in a special streaming program where we could complete two grades in one year. I took it as a challenge.

But after the fall, I couldn't do it. I wasn't able to compete. I just couldn't get interested again. I wasn't able to recall enough test answers. My mind wandered during class. And my next report card was nothing like the O's, A's, and B's of the year before.

"Mark (as I was known then) is just never ready for class," the teacher wrote. "His work and supplies are never in an orderly form. This is a handicap, and every effort should be made to correct a bad habit. He's enthusiastic and I enjoy having him in my class. In the last week, he has really tried to do neat, careful work. If this keeps up, he will improve."

I tried to improve, but it didn't work. The worst part about it was that from then on in school, it seemed that I was branded abnormal.

The first stigma was the special protective helmet I had to wear for three months after the accident. The other kids had a field day with the wisecracks—"Hey, general, where's the war?" I'd never been the most popular kid at school anyway because I got good grades and enjoyed getting special attention from teachers. I also liked to talk about my playing hockey and didn't mind doing a little bragging. Now my classmates made school an ordeal.

Even after the helmet came off, I still considered

myself a marked man. Everyone seemed to assume I was academically inferior. Whenever I'd begin a new grade, mom would have a talk with the teacher and explain about the accident. I was no longer in the advanced classes. I was put into the second class. It seemed that I'd been branded as someone who couldn't learn, who couldn't remember. In high school, I was put into the vocational program instead of the regular academic track. *It's not fair*, I thought. *Why can't I be given the same chance again?* No one seemed to expect me to do well in school anymore, and that bothered me.

One area, however, remained unaffected by the accident—my love for competition. Since I wasn't able to compete in the classroom anymore, suddenly all my competitiveness was concentrated on sports. I was determined to excel at something. I began to see competition as a huge mountain. I was determined to begin the ascent.

I knew that lots of kids dream of becoming famous athletes. Only a few ever come close. But I had something going for me that more than evened the odds—I had a father named Lloyd Hunter.

Three
MY FATHER'S SON

IF DETERMINATION, GRIT, AND HARD WORK were all it took to make dreams come true, all three of Lloyd Hunter's boys would have become professional hockey players.

Dad was an incurable hockey fan. When he was growing up, he wanted to play professional hockey, but his family couldn't afford the equipment and training necessary to allow him to compete seriously. But now that he owned a farm of about 640 acres, he had the means to give his boys the opportunity he had missed.

A tall, thin man, dad wore his hair combed back and sported bushy sideburns and a mustache even before it was fashionable. He enjoyed telling funny stories and wasn't above a practical joke—he thrived on attention. But when he was working, he was intense. He didn't like to waste time—even when he was having fun, he worked at it. Of the

three boys, I seem to have inherited more than my
share of those traits.

That kind of attitude toward work is a requirement, however, to run a farm. Raising wheat and
tending the cows was a whole-family affair. Dad
taught my brothers and me to drive tractors before
our legs were long enough to reach the pedals.
We'd climb onto the seat with dad, he'd start the
machine, put it in gear, and jump off, leaving us at
the wheel. All we had to do was steer. If we wanted
to stop, we could only jump onto the clutch with
both feet and wait for dad to come and take it out of
gear.

As far as he was concerned, there was no conflict
of interest between hockey and the farm. He
thought all work was good for the body. Nothing
could be better for growing boys than hard work. In
fact, he reasoned, farm labor was great conditioning for hockey. Soon the farm chores began to look
more and more like a training program.

Clare, Lorne, and I had to carry big five-gallon
pails of chop for the cattle. When we would come
home from school, all the chop still needed to be
moved and fed to the calves. Dad could easily have
moved it with a tractor, but he had us lug it around.
We later discovered that he considered this good
training.

Dad always made sure we had a place to skate. At
first, he just leveled off some ground, and when the
weather got cold enough, he watered it. But it
seemed like each year he added something. Before
long we had a regulation-size rink there on the

farm. It had boards, lines, nets, everything.

In Saskatchewan, the winter sun can disappear as early as three o'clock in the afternoon, which doesn't leave much after-school time. Our solution was to drive the car and the half-ton pickup truck to opposite corners of the rink and aim the headlights onto the ice. Then one year, dad even installed lights at the rink. I was amazed that he would do all this for three boys, but he was determined that we'd have the facilities to train properly. So Clare, Lorne, and I spent hours at a time skating, stick handling, and shooting pucks.

Then dad found a little book called *Let's Play Hockey*. He had never been short on training ideas before, but now everything was more organized than ever.

On winter mornings, we'd get up early and put on our skates, not shoes. We'd skate over to the barn, slip on the skate guards, milk the seventy-six cows, take off the skate guards, and skate back to the kitchen for breakfast. After making sure our schoolbooks were ready, we were back outside skating again. We weren't particularly keen about getting up early and milking cows, but we loved to skate. We'd stay out until we heard the school bus beeping its horn two miles down the road. Then we'd race like crazy back to the house, flip off our skates, put on our shoes, grab our books, and run a quarter of a mile down to the end of the lane to catch the bus. More than once, we missed it, and mom had to drive us to school.

When we came home from school, the skates

went back on, and we went back out on the ice with mom's good kitchen chairs (they weren't good when we got done with them). Lorne would sit on one, and I would push him the length of the ice. Then we'd switch. After ten or twenty times, we'd go milk the cows again. Before long, we realized we could cut our workout time in half if we both pushed chairs simultaneously. So we filled old twenty-pound cement bags with sand and set them on the chairs. Somehow the increased efficiency didn't reduce our time on the ice. We couldn't ever get in too much skating, and dad was always coming up with new drills for us to try. We didn't mind—we preferred skating to anything else anyway. We hurried through homework at night so we could get in some more skating before bed.

Dad also made sure we always had the best equipment. We probably had the first Bauer Supreme 91 skates in the town. We practiced with steel pucks to strengthen our shooting, passing, and handling. If we had been strong enough to lift those pucks off the ice with a shot, we could have broken someone's shin. But we managed to survive intact.

At Christmas, we always knew we were getting hockey gear. Dad would get a Christmas tree that went all the way to the ceiling, and underneath it would be a pile of wrapped boxes of all sizes and shapes. We knew it was hockey stuff, but we didn't know who was getting what—the boxes were unmarked. Mom and dad never put the tags on, because they knew once we found out which ones were for us, we'd start trying to peek. Patience has never been one of my virtues.

During the summers, dad would always send us to hockey camps. As we grew older, he gave us more and more time off from farm work so we could attend hockey camps. Some years we spent five weeks at different camps—some in British Columbia, some in Toronto, others closer to home—while mom, dad, and Marilyn were left with all the farm work.

Hockey and farming weren't the only interests in the Hunter family, however. Mom and dad made sure we developed in all areas of life. I learned to do a lot of reading, and because our family did lots of performing in churches, I learned to sing. Even more important, however, was the emphasis mom and dad put on spiritual things.

Often spiritual lessons were taught as the situation arose. I will never forget the incident of the quarters when I was eight. Dad always had an old shaving bowl sitting on the shelf at the head of his bed. At night, before hanging up his pants, he'd always take the change out of his pocket and put it in the bowl. For some reason, he'd take out the pennies, nickles, and dimes, but he always left the quarters. The bowl was invariably full of quarters.

"Now if I just nab a couple of those, he'll never know the difference," I said to myself. So one morning I slipped in and pocketed about ten of them. That whole day at school I was terrified. *Dad knows. He's going to find out. He's going to come and pull me right out of school*, I thought. But that didn't stop me from showing off the quarters to my classmates.

When I got home that night, dad didn't say anything about it, but I was still nervous. Had he discovered any coins missing? If he had, he didn't give any indication of it.

After supper, as I was changing clothes, I got careless. The quarters fell out of my pockets and jangled to the floor. I thought the clinking would never end.

Dad walked in the room and said, "What do you have in your pocket, Mark?"

"Money."

I knew I was found out, but I was determined to tell the biggest lie I could to sneak it by.

"Where'd you get it?"

"I found it at school."

"Where?"

"Well, you know where we play marbles on the west side of the school? I walked by there at noon today, and there they were."

"Could you show me where?" dad asked.

"Sure."

"Why don't we go tomorrow and have another look? Maybe there's more."

The next day, instead of riding the bus to school, I rode with dad. We walked past the swings to the pit where we played marbles. I showed him the hole.

"Right there. That's where the money was."

Dad shook his head and said, "There doesn't seem to be any today."

"No, I guess not."

Then he looked me right in the eye and said, "Why don't you tell me where you really got the money?"

There was always something about my dad, about that certain look in his eye, about his pointed questions, that made me totally afraid. I started to cry. Through my slobbering, tears, and runny nose, I told him what I'd done.

But the reason this incident is so vivid, I think, is that this was the one time dad didn't spank me. I knew I deserved it, and I was sure I was going to get walloped. But I didn't. Dad just took the money back, looked me in the eye, and sent me to class. He never mentioned the incident after that. I vowed to myself that I'd never steal or lie again.

It must have been all of three days before I was caught slipping jawbreakers into my coat sleeve down at the store. This time dad gave me a lot more than his look.

A couple of months later, a missionary came to the Masonic hall in Shaunavon for a week of meetings. Each night, he told stories about his work in some foreign country. I don't remember exactly where (my memory still has a few gaps). But it sounded like an adventure. The missionary also made me extremely uncomfortable. He told how the people with whom he worked would often lie and steal. I started to squirm.

When the missionary explained that people were going to be punished someday for sins like lying and stealing, I was downright miserable. I knew I was guilty.

But then he pointed out that people who ask God for forgiveness can be cleared of the consequences. He quoted a verse from the Bible, 1 John 1:9—"If we confess our sins, he [God] is faithful and just to forgive us our sins, and to cleanse us from all unrighteousness." I was listening.

At the end of the week of meetings, the missionary asked those who wanted to ask God for forgiveness to walk down to the front of the room. I went. The first and most important mountain in my life had been scaled. My sins, which separated me from God, were forgiven.

It wasn't just a guilty conscience that sent me up front, however. I also wanted to be a missionary. More than the adventure, I wanted to tell other people about forgiveness, about freedom from guilt.

I told the speaker, "I want to be a Christian, and I want to go to the mission field."

"That's wonderful, Mark. Someday you'll have the honor of doing the Lord's work."

"No, you don't understand," I said. "I want to go now."

"Now, Mark," the speaker said, "You're not old enough yet. But you will be someday."

Even at eight years old, I wasn't going to be denied. I said to myself, "I don't care—I'm going to go."

So while the missionary was packing up all his curios, I crawled into the back seat of his car and lay down on the floor. I hoped he wouldn't notice me until it was too late, and he'd have to take me to the mission field with him.

The missionary finished saying his good-byes, packed his materials in the trunk, and climbed behind the wheel. He never saw me. I was sound asleep.

About half a mile down the road, the bumping of the car woke me. I sat up and said, "What mission field are we going to?"

Apparently it wasn't too late. He turned the car around and returned his stowaway to the church. I thought my parents would be angry, but they were rather amused and impressed by my zeal. No doubt if I'd gone further than half a mile, however, the consequences would have been a bit more dire.

After that, my traveling was limited to summer hockey camps. Even though I didn't realize it, most of them could have qualified as mission fields. Some of them were pretty rough.

Clare, my older brother, gained something of a reputation as an enforcer. At one hockey school in Toronto, several of the bigger kids formed a gang and were beating up some of the smaller players. Clare, in typical Hunter style, acted without a second thought. He took on some of the big guys and whipped them. It didn't stop the gang tactics, but it made them less frequent.

All in all, I knew I was off to a great start as an athlete. Not every kid has the backing from his parents that I had. Unfortunately, it was in the wrong sport.

Four
EIGHT YEARS BEHIND

MOST WORLD CUP RACERS first start skiing when they are three or four years old. When I turned eleven, I still had never worn a pair of skis. The only boots I'd laced on had blades attached. To the flatland farmers in southwestern Saskatchewan, hockey was the proper winter pastime—skiing was as foreign as fresh fish.

Shaunavon, population 2,800, was a great place for growing wheat but not for raising Olympic skiers. Shaunavon's only claim to fame was its water. At the city limits stands a sign that reads, "Shaunavon—Home of the Queen's Water." Whenever the queen would visit Canada, a huge railroad tank car would stop in Shaunavon and fill up with soft, 99.9-percent-pure spring water. But water for the queen's bath is a little different from the frozen variety required to develop world-class ski racers.

So my skiing career already had two strikes against it before it ever began. First, I was already too old to entertain serious notions about skiing competitively. Many ski racing clubs don't accept kids over twelve years old. Second, our farm was 400 miles from the Rockies and skiable snow. All the factors seemed to be directing me toward hockey. There would have to be some extraordinary events to overcome an eight-year disadvantage and a hockey orientation to make me a skier.

In the fall of 1961, an issue of *Power for Living*, a Sunday school paper, had featured a story about the Christian philosopher Francis Schaeffer and his retreat center, L'Abri, in the Swiss Alps. Dad was so impressed he brought the paper home, read it to us, and saved it in his top drawer. He wistfully remarked how great it would be to have a chalet like that where we could combine skiing and sharing our faith.

Three years later, when neighbors Gordon and John Chandler invited dad and Clare to go skiing with them at Bear Paw Mountain in Montana, dad brought the paper out to read it again. He still had a dream of living near the mountains.

Lorne and I raised such a fuss about not being able to go to Bear Paw with dad that he had to promise to take us later on in the year. Ironically, on that first outing, seasoned skier Gordon Chandler broke his leg, while dad and Clare emerged unharmed and excited about skiing. Gordon's broken leg didn't dampen my enthusiasm to try the new sport. Lorne and I kept asking when dad was going to take us.

That Christmas, dad bought us skis, and our first introduction to skiing was being pulled around the farm by a rope attached to the horse. After several trips around the yard and along the ditches, we got tired of that.

"We can't go fast enough behind a horse," we complained. "Why don't we go behind the half-ton?"

So dad drove the pickup truck, and we'd take turns holding onto the forty-foot rope attached to the rear bumper. Dad drove along the roads, and we skied on the deep snow in the ditches. For pure enjoyment, being towed behind a half-ton rivals any of the ski slopes I've seen since.

If it was a sunny day and our goggles were on, everything was smooth. But if the day was overcast, we couldn't see the bumps. We'd hit a dip, which would throw us a little off balance. Then we'd run into a drift, the rope would yank taut, and we'd explode out of the drift into the air, coming to earth just in time to catch another drift. With a series of drifts, it was just a matter of time before we'd catch our tips in the snow, tumble headfirst and find our faces buried, eating the white stuff. We loved it.

Another thing we tried was the waterskiing technique. We'd pull around to the side of the truck, just missing the telephone poles along the road. Then we'd cut back across, catch a drift, jump over the road, and land on the other side. Once in a while, there wouldn't be enough snow on the approach, and we'd land right on the road—not a pleasant experience if the road had been cleared of snow.

To cut down the chances of gravel-face landings, dad suggested we build a ramp on our ice rink for jumping. So we did. Dad took down the boards at both ends of the rink and built two ramps parallel to each other, one on each side of the ice, made with milk cans and plywood. One ramp was two cans tall; the other was four cans tall. Then dad drove the half-ton down the lane, through the middle of the rink and between the two ramps. Forty feet later, at the end of the tow rope, we'd zip up the ramps at thirty miles an hour and fly into the air.

Flying off a six-foot ramp onto solid ice was a jarring experience. But after some experimentation, we discovered that covering the ice with snow and straw made a perfect landing area.

All this was major news in Shaunavon. We were considered weird by everyone else in town, but we rather enjoyed giving people that impression. It set us apart; we were different; we were noticed.

Most Sunday afternoons that winter were spent on the ramps. We hurried home from church, gobbled dinner, and put on our skis so we could jump all afternoon until milking time. By then we were so tired that milking the cows seemed like an endless ordeal. But we never thought of shortening our time on the jumps.

Eventually, however, the ramps began to seem tame. We wanted to hit the big slopes. The only place around Shaunavon even remotely resembling a ski slope was a gentle 200-foot hill on the Amon farm. Mrs. Amon thought it amusing that the three Hunter boys wanted to use her hill for skiing, and she generally had hot chocolate and cookies waiting for us when we were done. A road wound around the back of Amon's Hill to the top of the slope. We'd open the trunk of the car, sit facing backwards, and dangle our skis over the bumper. Dad would drive us to the top of the hill, let us off, then race us to the bottom—he in the car, we on our skis. We usually won.

Before long, dad decided we skied well enough to take us to a real mountain. We were also driving him to distraction with our eagerness to go. He planned a weekend trip to Montana. That Friday he told us not to get in any trouble at school. The border crossing at Bracken closed at 5:30, and school got out at 4:00. If we had to stay after school, we'd never make it. Amazingly, all three Hunter boys made it through Friday without any detentions. We ran to the car, and dad drove like mad to make it through Bracken.

That began our weekend skiing excursions. Mom and Marilyn would stay home to milk the cows, and Clare, Lorne, dad, and I would go. It didn't take long before we were sold on skiing, even though hockey remained our first love.

Over Easter vacation, 1965, we went skiing at Big Mountain in Whitefish, Montana.

Our favorite slope was one that was wide and straight, with some boulders at the bottom of the run. Since the boulders were covered with three feet of snow, Lorne and I decided to see who could jump off the biggest rock. First I went, and then Lorne. We bombed straight downhill, shot over the rocks, and launched ourselves into midair. Thirty feet beyond, we landed, made a quick stop, and immediately headed back uphill for another run.

Dad was standing at the bottom of the hill when Len Kaufman, the ski director at Big Mountain, walked up.

"I wonder whose kids those are," he said.

"Why?"

"Because those two boys should be in racing. They just scream down the hill. They have virtually no fear. Especially the big kid. He's the best skiing buffalo I've ever seen."

I was big for my age in those days, and rather chunky. I didn't have any style on skis, but I loved to go fast. When dad told me about Len Kaufman's buffalo description, I laughed, but had to admit it was probably pretty accurate.

My size and my love for speed got me into trouble more than once. One time at Whitefish, I raced to the lift line too fast and couldn't stop. I hit the lift shock and broke the tip of my ski. Dad was so mad that I thought I'd have to sit the rest of the holiday in the lodge. Instead, he bought me a pair of Head metal skis. From then on, nothing was going to stop me. Speed was what I was after, and the new Heads gave me more than enough.

From that time on, dad often took us skiing. I think he loved it, too. It didn't lessen his zeal for our hockey training, but he thought the two sports could complement one another. He figured ski racing as a recreational sport was a good way to train for hockey.

That summer after I turned twelve, dad realized that if we were really serious about hockey, Shaunavon was not the place to be. There simply wasn't enough competition. The bigger and better hockey players were in the cities. If we had a steady diet of tougher competition in the Peewee, Bantam, and Midget levels of amateur hockey, then we'd have a lot better chance of making Junior A hockey someday. And without a good experience in Junior A, it's almost impossible to play professional hockey.

Throughout the summer, dad checked out hockey programs. He visited Regina, Moose Jaw, Medicine Hat, Calgary, and Lethbridge, looking for a place that would give his boys the best opportunity to develop their hockey skills.

At that time, Moose Jaw, Medicine Hat, and Lethbridge didn't have Junior A level hockey. Regina and Calgary did, and dad's thoughts turned toward one of those two places. But he still wasn't sure if he wanted to move or not. Was it worth it?

Then one night in September, dad sat bolt upright in bed.

"Mom, let's get the kids packed. We're moving to Calgary."

Dad had made up his mind. Since Calgary was

closer to the mountains and skiing facilities, it was better than Regina. Even though we knew he'd been considering a move, it took us all by surprise. But we also knew that once dad had made up his mind, the only feasible thing for us to do was to do what he said. We started packing the next day. As I look back, I marvel at dad's courage. Leaving a small town isn't easy, but he boldly did what he thought was best for his boys.

So from then on, we lived in two homes. We kept the farm in Shaunavon and lived there in the summer to raise the crops. But the rest of the year, we lived in Calgary, went to school, played hockey, and skied. Mom started working at Foothills Hospital in Calgary. Dad and Marilyn stayed at the farm year-'round to tend the cows. Almost every weekend, mom would make the 600-mile round trip to visit dad and Marilyn.

That winter, I entered Colonel Irvine Junior High, played Bantam level hockey, and went skiing whenever I had a free night or weekend. Dad didn't want us getting into trouble, so he had given us a choice—ski or take ballet lessons. It wasn't a difficult choice.

On one of those free weekends, while skiing at Happy Valley near Calgary, I saw a slalom course that had been set up. I'd never tried slalom gates before, but figured there was no time like the present to see what they were like. I took a couple runs through them, and just as I was completing one, I saw a man waiting for me at the bottom. He skied over to me. I saw he had a pencil and paper.

"What's your name?" he said. It was more a statement than a question.

"Mark Hunter," I said, certain that I'd been caught doing something wrong.

"Where do you live?"

"6411 Travois Crescent, in Thorncliffe district."

"What's your phone number?"

It sounded like the third degree, and I was a little nervous. What had I done? I didn't know, but I didn't want to make him mad by refusing to answer.

He closed the interrogation with a cryptic "Okay, you'll be hearing from us."

Uh oh, I thought, *I'm in for it now. He'll call my parents, and I'll catch it when I get home.*

But that night when I got home, nothing happened. Nor did anything happen the next day. But the day after that, when I got home from school, there was a letter from Bob Pierce of the Calgary Skimeisters, inviting me to join. He had also called mom the same day and told her about Skimeisters. It was a volunteer club to promote ski racing and help young racers. About 150 kids were in the program. The Skimeisters invited me back for the rest of the Christmas camp at Happy Valley to try out and see how I liked it. Then if I wanted to join, I could.

Later, I discovered that there had been quite a bit of disagreement about inviting me to the camp. Some of the Skimeister coaches thought that twelve years old was too old to be starting to race. But eventually they decided to let me try out.

Naturally, I wanted to go to the camp. It turned out to be three days of nothing but training for slalom and giant slalom. We ran gates, ran gates, and ran gates. I was fascinated. I'd never done anything like that before. And I was amazed at how much technique was involved. There was a lot more to it than just skiing back and forth between poles.

I did find, however, that I had one advantage over some of the other kids. I wasn't scared to go full speed. Some of the others slowed themselves down on the turns to stay in control. I tried to go full speed and not lose any momentum.

At the end of the three days, the Skimeisters held a slalom race, and I won the Midget division. I noticed that a television film crew was there, so when I got home, the first thing I said was, "I'm going to be on television!"

We didn't have a TV then, so we went to the next-door neighbor's house to watch the news. Sure enough, it showed my run and the awards ceremony. I loved the individual recognition. It was something I'd never experienced before. Hockey had always brought team honor. With skiing, I was recognized for my achievement. It was a heady experience.

The next week, the Skimeisters held a downhill camp at Pigeon Mountain. After winning the slalom, nothing could have kept me away from this camp.

There wasn't a downhill race that weekend, but they did record practice times. Even though I was a little nervous, apparently the other kids were even more so, because I turned in the fastest time among my age group.

Immediately I was slated as a downhiller. Plenty of kids could ski a good slalom. But only people who are experienced or crazy can handle the downhill. Since I'd been skiing only a year and had been in my first race just a week ago, I knew I wasn't experienced. But I'd never been afraid of speed. That was probably the only thing that allowed me to compete with kids who had been skiing six or seven years.

Even though I didn't win another race for four years, that initial success changed my identity. The Skimeister coaches took my name—James Mark Hunter—from my birth certificate, and apparently they assumed I went by the first name. So on the slopes, I became Jim. I sort of liked it.

At home, at school, and in hockey, however, I was still Mark Hunter. Mark was continually getting in trouble at home. Mark had learning problems at school. Mark was "the country kid" whom the hockey players and coaches in Calgary seemed slow to accept. Mark was the one who had to wear a hockey helmet.

Jim Hunter didn't have to wear a helmet on the ski slopes (except in the downhill, where everyone did). Jim didn't have problems learning to ski. And when Jim competed, he didn't have to share the credit or blame with anyone but himself.

I began to see that more and more of me would become Jim, and less and less would remain Mark.

Five
MORE THAN COURAGE

SKIING IS A SIMPLE SPORT—or so I thought when I first started racing. All you have to do is strap a couple of slick boards to your feet and go from the top of the mountain to the bottom as fast as you can. The only requirement is not to break anything except previous records. Overcoming fear is the only obstacle—and that had never been too much of a problem for me.

It didn't take long to learn that there's more to skiing than skiing itself. Courage and a reckless love for speed had been enough to win at lower levels of competition, but I soon discovered I needed something else for the higher levels.

After one year with the Skimeisters, dad realized that if I really wanted to be a ski racer, I'd need more instruction than I could get at weekend camps. So in the summer of 1966, he agreed to send me to my first ski camp at Red Lodge, on the slopes of Mount Hood in Oregon. That ten-day camp was my introduction to the real world of ski racing.

All of a sudden, I learned that ski preparation and physical conditioning were just as important as on-the-slope technique.

Pepi Stiegler, a 1964 Olympic gold medal winner, was one of the Red Lodge instructors. I watched Pepi and the other instructors and picked up some of the finer points of ski technique, but it seemed I was always tired. Despite my summers of wrestling haybales and pails of chop, and winters of pushing cement bags around the ice on mom's chairs, I was exhausted after a day of racing.

At the end of the ten days, the comments on the back of my diploma read, "Jim has a lot of ability and a lot of strength, but he lacks energy and conditioning."

When I got home and showed that to my dad, he looked at me and said, "I'm going to whip you into shape." Then the training became serious.

Dad did something that only later struck me as significant—he bought me 300 pounds of barbells. Looking back, I don't know if he really expected a thirteen-year-old kid to lift them all at once, but it showed something of his expectations.

Then dad started buying cans of Protein 101 and Formula Number Seven, two high-protein diet supplements. I had to mix the stuff with milk and drink it. The ads claimed it would make me look like the muscle men in the magazines. I believed it and downed the potion religiously.

Later dad started making a homemade concoction after reading an article in a sports magazine about a young Olympic hopeful named Mark Spitz who ate the stuff to build the muscles he needed for swimming. It was a mixture of peanut butter, honey, rose hip powder, gelatin, ice cream, milk, bananas, and a few other things dad decided to throw in. It was called *glop*. If it doesn't sound very appetizing, it wasn't. Dad would mix it up in gallon pails and put it in the freezer.

Every meal he'd want us to eat some. It tasted like peanut butter ice cream, but the consistency was more like a mangled banana. It wasn't too bad when it was frozen, but if it was warm, it was revolting.

With the weights and diet supplements, dad designed a program that became a daily routine. At first I hated it. As soon as I came in from the field, dad would say, "Let's go. Barbells, right now. If you're going to get that fat off, you've got to work."

I would mumble something about being tired, but I knew it was useless to argue. I'd go through the routine while dad mixed the Protein 101. Dad had charts on the wall listing each exercise, and I had to mark them off as I did them. We also kept a scale in the room. I was hefty for my age, and dad wanted me to lose weight.

When I started, I weighed 120 pounds. After one week, I dropped to 110.

"C'mon, you've got to make 105," dad said.

A couple weeks later, I was down to 105.

"You've got to get down to 100," dad insisted.

I thought I was going to waste away to a mere shadow, but I didn't. What was happening was that all the fat was being shed.

When I got to 100 pounds, dad said, "I think you can go down five more pounds."

I tried for two more weeks to get down to 95. I got down to 98, but I couldn't get any lower. There wasn't an ounce of fat left—I was the skinniest thirteen-year-old you'd want to see.

The pictures on the wall of Harold Pool, Larry Scott, and the other muscle men looked ludicrous next to me. I was supposed to be doing the same routines they followed, but my beanpole body bore no resemblance to theirs.

After two weeks of remaining at 98 pounds, I was ready to give it up. I didn't care any more. The fat was off, but so what? Was it worth all the sweat, the aching muscles, and the boring repetitions? Worst of all was the mental energy it took to convince myself to bear down and exert.

Dad started reading me stories about Gordie Howe when he was growing up in Floral, Saskatchewan. Gordie would run to school, racing the bus. I knew what was coming. A new wrinkle was added to my training program—running. At first it was just to the end of the lane and back—a half mile. Gradually we increased the distance. Dad had me run behind the cultivator and tractor as he drove through the fields.

All of a sudden, I got on the scale at the end of the week, and I weighed 106 pounds! I couldn't believe it. What had happened? I looked in the mirror and was amazed. I'd started to bulk out. I could see my pectoral muscles developing, and there was some definition in my biceps.

From that time, working out was never again a problem of motivation. I'd made visible progress, and now I was convinced I could look like Harold Pool. I was determined to be a muscle man and never be accused of being out of shape again.

At the end of the summer, the 1966 FIS World Championships were held in Portillo, Chile. Nancy Greene was the top Canadian skier. She hadn't become a big winner yet, but I knew she was on her way up. She'd placed seventh in the downhill at the 1964 Olympics at Innsbruck, and fifth in the downhill in the 1962 World Championships at Chamonix, France.

Nancy didn't place in the downhill at Portillo, but she did finish fourth in the giant slalom. That fall, a movie about the World Championships came to Calgary. It was called *The Secret Race*. Our whole family went to see it, and I fell in love with Nancy Greene. Not only her wholesome beauty but her aggressive skiing attracted me. She didn't hold anything back. Her skiing was hard, fast, and furious—just the way I wanted mine to be.

When I got home, I sat down and wrote three love letters to her. I never mailed them, but I was infatuated. She was young, Canadian, and without fear.

From then on, I was inspired. I'd seen what skiing could be like, and I was determined to imitate it. My thoughts centered on how I could improve my skiing, Whenever I went down a flight of stairs, I wouldn't simply walk down—I'd practice my slalom technique by jumping side to side down each stair.

Mom told someone that "everyone else wears out the carpet down the middle of the stairs. Jim wears it out on either side."

Up until now, I'd still been doing both hockey and skiing. But I was starting to feel the pressure to choose between the two. My hockey coach told me that skiing wasn't good for my hockey—the risk of injury, the distraction, and the conflict of interest were detrimental to my development as a hockey player. The coaches of the Skimeisters told me the same thing—"If you're serious about skiing, you ought to forget hockey."

It wasn't a snap decision—more of a gradual process—yet slowly but surely, I felt myself drawn toward skiing and away from hockey.

I had always had the courage, and now I had the conditioning and the inspiration. I was sure that was the winning formula. What could possibly stand between me and skiing success?

As it turned out, quite a few things.

Six
NOT GOING TO TAKE IT ANYMORE

ONE OF THE THINGS that has gotten me into trouble throughout my life has been my need to be noticed. No matter what the activity, I have enjoyed being the center of attention.

In Shaunavon, it was rather easy to get attention—there wasn't much competition. Even after the fall on the basement floor and the loss of my ability to impress the teachers academically, I still managed to be a prominent personality— hockey and the skiing stunts saw to that.

After we moved to Calgary, however, the job was a lot tougher. There were more people, better hockey players, and fewer friends who knew of my previous reputation. I didn't seem to make many friends readily in Calgary, so I went to great lengths to impress my new classmates and teachers. Sometimes it required doing some offbeat things.

For instance, I often wore a suit and tie to school, and I usually carried a briefcase with a Bible inside. It was my way, admittedly an immature and superficial way, of showing people I was a Christian. I wanted people to see I was different. I may not have succeeded in communicating my faith effectively, but my goal of being noticed was a huge success.

I was also the only boy in the Colonel Irvine Junior High Glee Club. Our family has always been musical—dad played the saxophone and often directed church choirs, and our family frequently traveled to camps and different churches to present a musical program. I learned to sing when I was very young, but a love of music was not the reason I joined the glee club. I joined because no other boy had ever done it.

The glee club idea worked out better than I ever dreamed it would. The director was so pleased to have a boy in the group that she decided to take advantage of it. She gave me a number of solo parts with the girls singing background. I got the attention I was after, but it also served to infuriate the other guys in school.

Getting pushed around, and occasionally beat up, was not unusual. I was different—a country kid, a religious nut, a show off. But worse, I thrived on being different—I chose to emphasize the distinctives.

Tact was not my strong point. Whenever I heard someone swear, I immediately said, "You shouldn't say that."

More times than not, the response was "Why the hell not?"

"Well, God's name is special. It's sacred. It's wrong to use it that way."

Beyond that, I couldn't think of anything else to say, and I invariably lost the arguments. Most guys didn't think much of my opinions anyway, because modesty was about as big with me as tact. I told a lot of hockey and skiing stories with myself as the main character. Most of them were true. But my listeners were unimpressed.

"I'm going to be in the Olympics," I predicted. "Someday I'll be a world champion." That, of course, isn't a hit tune with junior highers.

"Prove it" was the reply. "Let's see how tough you are." But I refused to fight. I didn't tell anyone about my cracked skull, even though it was still something I couldn't forget. Even when someone shoved me around, I wouldn't fight back—I just tried to get away.

Many afternoons, I would stay after school until 5:30, reading or toying with the piano. I told my parents I was doing extra work. But I wasn't. I was waiting for David Ebsen and his friends to leave. They were the ones who seemed to enjoy ridiculing my claims of eventual athletic greatness, and they often waited at the bike racks to shove me around. I dreaded having to face them, and they knew it. They also knew I didn't fight back. I wasn't like Lorne, who dished out more than he got, even when he tangled with bigger kids. I didn't want to give them the satisfaction of seeing me struggle. If it came to a fight, I said, "Go ahead and beat me up. I'm not going to hit anybody."

"You're chicken, Hunter."

"I'm not chicken," I said, but I knew I was. Down

deep I wasn't sure if I really believed any of my claims. Would I make it to the Olympics? I really didn't know.

Then about three weeks before the end of school, Lorne asked me, "Why don't you show those guys that you're as tough as you claim to be? You talk, but you never prove it. You're big enough to defend yourself."

"Aw, I don't want to."

But the next day in shop class, David Ebsen went through his ritual of wisecracks about how great I was going to be. I thought to myself, *I can't take this anymore. I'm not staying after school to avoid Ebsen any longer. If there's going to be a showdown, let's have it.*

For the rest of the week, however, nobody was waiting for me at the bike racks. I rode home unmolested, but not in peace. My stomach was tense. I wanted to get this over with. Finally on Friday afternoon, I got on my bike and rode down to the corner of the school where I knew David and his friends would be hanging around.

I rode right up to the group, got off my bike, and faced him. He was a little bigger than I was, but I tried to look him in the eye.

"I can't take any more of your guff," I said. "You've given me a hard enough time, and I'm not going to take it." I swung my right fist and punched him in the face. I'd never done anything like that before in my life. He was so surprised, he just stood there a second. It felt good. It was as if for once in my life I'd done something on my own, and I knew

I was going to prove what I'd been claiming.

Before he could recover, I hit him again and wrestled him to the ground, trying to hit his head against the dirt. Then I stopped. What do you do when you've got a guy down? I looked around and realized his friends were grinning and yelling. They looked pleased that he was finally getting the worst of it. I still didn't know what to do next. Do I let him up? *No,* I thought, *it would be stupid to give up the advantage I've got now.* So I started hitting him again.

Fortunately by that time, Mr. Chase, the literature teacher, had seen the ruckus from his classroom window and had come running out to break it up. Mr. Chase pulled me off David, who wasn't hurt but incredibly surprised and enraged.

After that confrontation, much of the harassment at school stopped. David and I never became friends, but he left me alone, and that was an improvement. As I look back, a schoolyard fight isn't something I'm particularly proud of now, but it was the beginning of a new attitude in me. That confrontation was the first proof I ever had that I could do what I'd only talked about before. For the first time I could see the benefit of my physical training. For the first time I saw that I *could* stand up for my convictions. I had a new, truer confidence.

If I could handle these guys, then maybe my other dreams could come true. Maybe those outlandish statements I'd been making about the Olympics weren't so outlandish after all.

Seven
TOUGHNESS AND TECHNIQUE

SKIING IS SUPPOSED TO BE A WINTER SPORT. Yet strangely enough, the best thing that ever happened to my skiing career happened during two summers. It was the camp at Kokanee Glacier that finally convinced me that my future was in skiing rather than hockey. It also added two new ingredients—toughness and technique—to my formula for winning that I was so desperately trying to perfect.

The hockey-skiing conflict came to a head early in the spring of 1967, and I knew I'd have to make a decision. The Triwood Provincial B hockey team played a game and the Skimeisters had a race—all on the same weekend. On Friday night, I scored three goals, and the hat trick helped our team win. On Saturday, I raced the Skimeister competition, and though I didn't win, I did well enough to get my name in the paper.

A MAN AGAINST THE MOUNTAIN

The Calgary Monday paper carried both stories on the same page, one above the other. My name was mentioned in each—Jim Hunter skiing and Mark Hunter playing hockey. When my hockey coach saw it, he told me I was foolish to ski and risk an injury that would ruin my hockey career. My skiing coaches also saw both stories and told me I needed to choose between the two—it's better to specialize in one area and be excellent than to be pretty good in two.

When you're only nearing your thirteenth birthday, it's tough to decide which sport you're going to devote the rest of your sporting life to. But realizing that the coaches had valid points, and realizing that I was costing my parents too many headaches and too much money by competing in two sports, I weighed the pros and cons of each. On one hand, hockey was the sport I'd been playing since I was old enough to skate. On the other hand, I enjoyed ski racing more—the credit or blame for my results lay solely on me, and I liked that feeling of personal responsibility. I also felt more accepted on the ski slopes. In hockey, my style of play set me apart. Dad had taught us a free-wheeling, let-her-rip style, like the Russians. In Calgary, the coaches in the younger-age leagues always wanted us to set up and have our attack organized before heading up the ice. Lorne and I hated that approach—it was like telling the other team what you were going to do. Consequently, Lorne and I weren't good team players, so we spent a lot of time on the bench.

Since summer camps were coming up soon, dad

and I sat down to decide which ones I'd go to. After talking it out, we decided that this summer I'd concentrate on skiing, just to see if that's what I really wanted. Dad let me make up my own mind and said he would support me in whichever sport I chose.

The Kokanee Glacier camp was sponsored by the Canadian national ski team. Two ten-day boys' camps were followed by two ten-day girls' camps, and then the best racers from each camp were invited back for a final mixed camp.

Kokanee is located in the Selkirk Mountain range near Nelson, British Columbia, almost directly north of the Washington-Idaho border. Our base camp was over 5,000 feet above sea level, and we looked up all around us at peaks between 8,000 and 9,000 feet. The glacier snow never completely melted. It was an isolated camp, accessible only by foot or by helicopter. Bears and porcupines would sometimes wander into camp and scavenge through the garbage pile. The only telephone was forty-five minutes away at the top of the mountain. It was a rugged setting, and a rugged experience. It was also the best thing that ever happened to my skiing.

Looking back, it's too bad that kids today don't have summer camps like Kokanee. At Kokanee Glacier, there was nothing but you, the snow, and the mountain. Coaches Larry Nelles, Jean Pierre Picher (whom we called Jeep), Butch Boutry, and Guy Christie had an opportunity for an intensive ten days of training and teaching technique. With-

Jim spends a quiet moment with his mother.

Gathered around the piano are (l. to r.) Lorne, Jim, Gail (now Jim's wife), dad, and Clare.

Fourteen-year-old Jim Hunter works on technique at Kokanee Glacier. . . .

Seven years later, during summer training at Whistler Mountain, B.C., he's still at it.

out the distractions of television, pool halls, and junk food, they managed to cram in an awful lot of coaching.

Unlike the summer before, I was in shape for Kokanee. Dad's training program started to pay off. Thanks to the weight lifting, diet supplements, and running, I was a solid 136 pounds and had a newly gained stamina. From the place where the road ended, it was a five-mile hike around a frozen lake and a pine-covered ridge to reach the camp. Each camper had to carry his pack that distance—only the skis and food were flown in by helicopter. When two of the other campers started tiring about halfway around the lake, I agreed to carry their packs. I wasn't even breathing hard. When I arrived at the camp carrying three packs and not feeling tired, I knew this was going to be a much better experience than last summer.

Base camp sat at the foot of the glacier. It was just a cluster of white canvas tents on wooden frames. Each tent had a wooden floor and contained eight bunks and a wood-burning stove.

When the first camp was held, early in June, snow still covered the ground almost fifteen feet deep all around the base camp. By August, it would have disappeared and the rocks and greenery would appear for a couple of months before the snow would cover them again.

Each morning and afternoon we had physical training—push-ups, sit-ups, and rope skipping. The coaches were constantly pushing us to beat the records set at earlier camps. We knew there would be a graded fitness test on the last day of camp that we'd need to be in top shape for.

Then, wearing either our ski boots or running shoes, and carrying our ski equipment, we hiked a mile and a half from the base camp to the ski lift there on the glacier. The rest of the morning was spent racing. We stopped for lunch but attacked the hill again immediately afterwards until the middle of the afternoon. From then until supper, we had free time. Since we were miles away from any diversion, we had to create our own.

One of the favorite pastimes was pouring some of the naphtha gas from the lanterns into the wood-burning stoves, replacing the stove lid, and then sticking a match into the hole at the bottom of the stove. The stove would almost blow apart. A flame would shoot up, and the explosion would send the lid flying all the way to the top of the tent. We were sure one of the times it would go all the way through, but it never did.

The coaches, of course, outlawed all this, but we continued anyway, usually three or four times a day. Finally, they started giving us only two days' supply of naphtha. If we ran out before the next allotment, we couldn't get any more. But even that didn't slow us down. Going without light was a small price to pay for such spectacular entertainment.

Discipline for other offenses was more severe. The most creative form of torture was reserved for the camp bully or any other racer who was convicted of being a brat. The coaches thought of the idea, but the campers administered it. We would wait until the offender was asleep in his sleeping bag; then someone would quietly zip the bag all the way up, and three or four guys would pounce.

We'd shove his head completely into the bag and tie the top tightly shut with string. By this time the victim was completely awake and usually very active, but a zipped and tied sleeping bag is an effective restraint.

The enforcers would pick up the sleeping bag, take their prey outside, and set him down right next to the stream. It was like Chinese water torture. He's inside the sleeping bag, he can't get out, and it sounds like he's being put in the water. The victim invariably went nearly berserk trying to get out of the bag, knowing that any minute he could be rolled into the icy stream. We'd just leave him there for ten minutes or so.

It effectively ended the troublemaking from that individual. Fortunately, I was never singled out as that serious of a problem child.

The stunt I was involved in, however, was a beauty. Four of us decided to try to jump over the cookshack. Without anyone knowing what we were doing, we started piling up snow on the backside of the cookshack until we had a ramp we were satisfied with—five feet high.

The next afternoon when everyone left the hill, the four of us stayed behind until the others reached camp—we wanted an audience. Then we came screaming down the glacier and swooped toward the cookshack. I hit the ramp just like my brothers and I had done on the milk-can ramps on the ice rink in Shaunavon. Pushing off as I came to the top of the ramp, I sailed over the tent and landed on the other side.

All four of us landed safely in front of our sufficiently surprised and impressed audience. It was one of the few times I ever saw the coaches startled. What we didn't know, however, was that Jeep Picher was behind us. He followed us down the hill, not knowing about the ramp.

At the last second, he realized what was happening and tried to stop. It was a mistake. He was going too fast and was too far committed to bail out now. He went off the ramp, but came down too early, landing right on top of the tent, crashing to the ground, and destroying four banana creme pies the cook had just set out for supper. Jeep wasn't hurt, but he made sure the ramp was knocked down before we ate that night.

The greatest thing I took away from Kokanee Glacier, however, was a new understanding of the mental and physical toughness required to be a winner. Two men were primarily responsible—Jeep Picher and Larry Nelles. These two coaches were, for me, the embodiment of toughness.

When he wasn't surprised by cookshack jumps, Jeep had an uncanny ability to make me put out everything I had. Normally, he was quiet and reserved and suffered from asthma attacks. But when he got into the clear, cold air at Kokanee, he came to life. He was a human avalanche. If I thought I could do seventy-five push-ups in a minute, Jeep would inspire me to do eighty-five. Through a skillful blend of intimidation, encouragement, and example, he convinced me that skiing was a barely contained explosion down a hill. Nothing else mattered but speed.

Larry Nelles inspired me to be physically tough, mostly because he was. Even though he was thirty-eight years old, he could do more push-ups, sit-ups, and rope skips per minute than anyone else in camp. He got me started running at five-thirty in the morning. He seemed to take a special interest in me and woke me up to go running with him. He would also line up a couple of us, Wayne Colborne and me, with our backs against a wall, hands shoulder high, and he would slowly move along the wall, shadow boxing. Bobbing and weaving, he'd gradually work his way to where we stood with our hands and backs pressed against the cement wall. Suddenly he'd jab three times, faster than I'd believed anyone could, and each one just barely touched my palm. Then he'd dance directly in front of me and direct those lightning-fast punches at my nose, stopping just short. Then he'd move on to my other palm and on to Wayne. If either of us flinched, we had to do fifty push-ups. It wasn't long before we both learned to look steadily at the coach as he jabbed at us.

Nelles also enjoyed telling about the days "when skiing was tough," in other words, when he was still competing. He told us about racing when he didn't have any transportation to get from one race to another, so he'd look for a train heading the right direction. Then he'd run after it, spot an open car, toss his skis in, climb in after them, and ride the boxcar all the way to the next race.

We all had a lot of respect and appreciation for Nelles. From knowing him, I learned discipline, control, and the ability to ignore distractions that interfered with my concentration on the mountain.

After that ten-day camp, I returned home feeling like I was really learning what it took to be a winner.

During the following school year, Skimeister coaches Ken Marchand and Ed Novotni became like second parents. They kept me in training, and tried to keep me humble. The first was easy, the second almost impossible.

"Jim, you have everything it takes to be a champion like Killy, except one thing," Marchand told me once. I fell for it.

"What's the one thing?"

"A little humility."

I was used to it by this time, though. I was constantly telling people that I'd be in the Olympics someday. Other times I'd challenge someone to a race and make a point of predicting by how many seconds I'd beat him. I wasn't modest, but then I figured if you could back up what you said, you didn't have to be modest.

Eight
JUNGLE JIM

ONCE I FINALLY DECIDED that skiing was my sport, all my energy was devoted to becoming a better ski racer than anyone else. It was this fervor, coupled with some unusual circumstances during my second summer at Kokanee Glacier, that earned me a permanent nickname.

After the first summer at Kokanee Glacier, I began keeping extensive training notes—how many miles I ran, the number of sit-ups and push-ups done, my pulse rate, my weight, and what I ate. Every night, I faithfully recorded into my notebook everything that I thought might have an effect on my skiing.

During the winter, when I started skiing every weekend, I added diagrams of each of the race courses to my notebook. I drew the position of each of the poles, noted snow conditions and bumps, and marked the most difficult sections of the run.

I also became an avid fan of ski movies. Slow-motion is the best way to study technique, since you can see body position, weight shifting, the pole plant, skis flexing, and the edges biting into the snow. *The Secret Race*, featuring Nancy

Greene, and *The Last of the Ski Bums* made an indelible impression on me. They were my inspiration for many years. Often as I would be riding up a lift, I'd look around at the snow and trees, but I wouldn't see them—I'd be visualizing the slow-motion scenes from the movies, fluid turns, hips brushing the gate, and snow flying.

The next summer, when I was fifteen, I returned to Kokanee Glacier determined to be invited to the mixed camp. Dad arranged for me to attend both sessions of the boys' camp. My intense training started to pay off. The two-mile runs around the lake, the fitness tests, and the skiing all seemed to be a little easier this year. Unlike that first summer at Red Lodge, I wasn't dragging along. I was usually the first person up the mountain to the ski lift every morning and one of the last to leave.

After the first camp, I was reasonably satisfied with my progress. I seemed to be doing as well as anyone else in camp. But simply doing well and being in shape didn't guarantee that I'd be invited to the mixed camp. That was a group decision of the coaches, based on some intangible qualities such as competitiveness, coachability, and most wispy of all—something called potential. Of necessity, it was a subjective decision—there wasn't any other way. So I couldn't let down.

There was a three-day break before the next ten-day camp, but since I didn't have the money or means to get home, I stayed at Kokanee over the break. I didn't mind—it was an opportunity to get in some additional skiing at no extra charge.

The trouble at the second session of camp was that the weather didn't cooperate. The first few days were fine—clear and cold—and we were able to train, but then the clouds moved in. It started to drizzle. Snow became so slushy and heavy that the coaches decided it was too dangerous to ski. Legs are broken more often in slushy snow because skis are harder to maneuver. So everyone sat around the tents, playing cards, waiting for the weather to break, and generally getting depressed.

I've never been able to sit still very long anyway, and sitting still inside a tent was more than I could bear. There had to be something better to do, and I decided to find it. Even one day off was too many for me.

If the snow wasn't any good for skiing, it had to be good for something. Why not sledding? Better yet, why not bobsledding? We could use the old safety toboggan we used for hauling wood. I went outside, grabbed a shovel, and hiked over to the hill. It wasn't raining too hard, actually only misting. I started slogging away with the shovel, digging out a bobsled run. It took the rest of the afternoon just to mark out the basic course. I was nowhere near finished when it got too dark to continue.

The next day was still overcast and raining, and skiing was cancelled again. So I headed back out to my bobsled run. About midmorning, Reto Barrington, one of the guys in my tent, came wandering over.

"What are you doing?"

"Building a bobsled run."

"What for?"

"Well, I'm not going to sit in a tent all day and get out of shape. I've got to keep busy."

So Reto started helping me. The rest of the day was a bobsled version of Tom Sawyer painting the white picket fence. One by one, other guys wandered over and started helping.

"Want some help?" they'd ask.

"Naw, I can do it," I said, which seemed to be more effective in getting them involved than eagerly inviting them to help.

Soon we had ten guys working on the run. We had five-foot banked turns. We built in a couple of jumps and rolls. It was a masterpiece. And the idea seemed to catch everyone's imagination.

We chose up teams and had time trials and then staged a tournament. Even the coaches got involved. We had both three- and four-man competition. Two full days were spent racing on that run until the toboggan finally broke in half. Fortunately, the next day the sky cleared, and we could ski again.

That session of camp, despite the weather, was talked about by those guys for years. "The bobsled camp" is remembered as one of the greatest ski camps we've ever been to.

At the end of the second boys' session, I asked Jackie Creed, who was directing the camp staff, if I could stay on through the girls' camps and work as a flunky. Flunkies are the semipaid helpers who cut wood, bring in the water, and serve food. They aren't involved in the ski training, but they can use their free time to practice on the glacier.

When I made my plea, I tried to make it sound like I was just trying to be Mr. Nice Guy, but I had an ulterior motive. What I really wanted was to be able to stay through the summer so I could be available for the mixed camp if I should be picked. I had fears that if I went home, the coaches wouldn't pick me. Or worse yet, they would pick me, but dad wouldn't be able to afford to send me back. I didn't want anything to happen to jeopardize my chances.

Luckily, one of the other flunkies decided he didn't want to stay at Kokanee anymore. When he went home, Jackie Creed said I could stay if it was okay with my parents. Together we climbed to the top of the mountain where the telephone was. We called the camp headquarters in Nelson, and they called dad to tell him what the situation was. Dad said it was fine to stay.

Pretty much throughout my life, mom and dad have been willing to let me have whatever I asked for. They were firm in their discipline, but they let me make many of my own decisions, especially things related to skiing. I wondered about that sometimes. I couldn't tell if mom and dad really wanted me to do it or not. At times I wished they'd just tell me what to do, instead of saying, "It's your decision." But I was sure of their love, and I was pretty sure they wanted me to be the best skier I could be, so I took the steps I deemed necessary to become a serious competitor. I deemed it necessary to be a flunky for the next two camps. So a flunky I became.

It was this experience that began a chain of events that led to my nickname. When the first girls' camp began, I'd already been at Kokanee Glacier for twenty-six days, and the isolation was beginning to affect me. There was absolutely no entertainment except what you could create for yourself—no bowling alleys, no hamburger joints. I had to do something about it before I went stir-crazy.

So I started concocting my own diversions. I decided to be a one-man welcoming committee for the girls. During the three days off, we flunkies rigged a rope to the high branch of a tree near the trail. As the girls hiked in, I jumped off a cliff near the trail, swung from the rope, landed on the trail, and yelled, "Welcome to Kokanee Glacier!"

The response wasn't overwhelming. But from then on, everyone remembered me for that stunt. If someone didn't recognize the name Jim Hunter, the only identification needed was "You know . . . the guy who thinks he's Tarzan."

Beyond that, things were fairly routine during the girls' camps—too routine for my tastes—but I was living for an invitation to the mixed camp. And sure enough, during the second girls' camp, I got it. Even though I'd been dreaming about this invitation, it still took me by surprise. The full impact struck me—I was only in my third year of racing, and now I'd be skiing with some of the national team members.

As it turned out, I wasn't very intimidated by the experience. For one thing, all my old cronies were back—Reto Barrington, Mike and Derek Robbins, and Mike Culver. For another thing, I'd been at Kokanee all summer, and it was practically like home; in fact it was almost too familiar.

There were two sides to my personality at that time. One was the stunt man, the Jim Hunter who played Tarzan, built bobsled runs, and jumped the cookshack. That Jim Hunter was more or less respected.

The other Jim Hunter was not. He was the religious kid, the one who said it was wrong to swear and tell dirty jokes. Some of the guys, when they got away from their parents, would buy a *Playboy* magazine and smuggle it into camp. The second Jim Hunter would say, "You shouldn't look at that trash."

The second Jim Hunter took a lot of static from the other racers. Looking back, I realize I brought most of it on myself, but at the time, it made me upset. *Why can't they see I'm right?* I thought. *I'm tired of being ridiculed for something that means a lot to me.*

One night in the tent, it seemed to be Pick-on-Jim-Hunter Night. And I'd had all I could handle.

"All right, that's it," I said. "I'm not going to take any more of this." I grabbed my sleeping bag and stalked out of the tent. I spent the night under a tree. It wasn't until the next day that I thought about the bears that occasionally visited the camp and could have made a meal of me.

Before I'd come to Kokanee, dad had bought me a styrofoam safari hat. "You'll need something to keep the sun off your head when you hike in and out of camp," he said.

When I got back to the tent after my night out, I noticed my safari hat had been tampered with—it had teeth marks all around the brim. Every kid in the tent, I discovered, had taken the hat and sunk his teeth into it, then passed it along. For some reason, the prank struck me as funny. I just laughed. My tentmates were a little miffed that I wasn't upset.

When they saw that the teeth marks hadn't made an impression (so to speak), they started scrawling obscenities on the hat. It wasn't long before I had to throw it away.

So it was a strange mixture of scorn and respect that I lived with during the mixed camp. When I was on skis, or when we were training, the respect was more evident. At night in the tent, the scorn and harassment emerged.

The incident that actually conceived the nickname began when someone dared me to swim across the small lake where we bathed. Actually we didn't bathe—it was too cold. We splashed a little water on our faces and upper bodies and hurriedly toweled off. Icebergs still dotted the lake, even in August. We shivered and shook all the way back to the tents.

But icebergs or no, I was never one to turn down a dare. Immediately I jumped in the water and began swimming across. In the middle of the lake was a rock, half-covered with ice, sticking above the surface. I swam to the rock, climbed up, turned around to look at the audience that had gathered on the shore, and then dived off the other side of the rock to swim to the far shore. There I turned around and swam all the way back, detouring around the rock.

As I climbed out of the water and dried myself off, I tried to sound nonchalant. "See? I told you I could do it." But I think my blue lips betrayed my bravado.

The onlookers, however, were incredulous. They just shook their heads and muttered. Words like *lunatic, hare-brained,* and *beyond hope* were the more understated expressions. I think it was Mike Culver who first said, "Well, that's Jungle Jim."

Judging by the way the nickname caught on, it seems amazing that no one had thought of it sooner. Before the camp ended, everyone was calling me Jungle, and the name has followed me ever since.

The name was important to me. It caught the personality I was trying to become. It reflected the first Jim Hunter, the stunt man, and that sure beat snide comments about my life-style and religious beliefs. I also felt it was an indication that other people saw the physical and mental toughness I was working to develop. I saw it as another step toward becoming a winner.

Nine
THE SWORD OF THE LORD

ONE OF THE REASONS I was so proud of being called Jungle was because of something that happened just before I went to Kokanee Glacier in 1968. It was something that made winning more important than ever.

While our family lived in Calgary, we attended Center Street Evangelical United Brethren Church. In the spring, evangelist Joel Rogers came for a week of revival meetings. Every night, Rogers preached that Jesus Christ should be preeminent, the primary concern in an individual's life. He said that everything else in life is secondary—only God's work should occupy the highest place in our lives.

Like those meetings seven years before in Shaunavon, I was deeply moved. My thoughts turned to my skiing. Despite my willingness to openly display my religion, I had to admit that it wasn't the most important thing in my life—skiing was. Or more precisely, winning was. I was bothered by Rogers's way of putting things— couldn't you live for two causes? Rogers insisted that either people lived for God, or they lived for themselves. There was no middle ground. "No man can serve two masters," said Rogers, quoting Matthew 6:24. Each night, I went home to do a lot of thinking.

Finally on the last night of meetings, Rogers pointed his comments directly at the young people. As he closed, he asked people to come forward if they were willing to open their lives to Jesus Christ's complete direction, to totally dedicate themselves to live according to his teachings.

I knew what I had to do. I loved skiing, but I didn't want it to come between me and God. I was ready to give it up if that's what God wanted.

About six of us went forward that night to indicate we were rededicating ourselves to serve God. It was a big decision, a conscious choice to place skiing under a higher call.

When our family got home that night, we sat around the kitchen table, munching cookies and talking about what had happened. Dad pointed out that serving God didn't mean I had to give up skiing. Instead, skiing could actually be my means of serving God—I could ski for God's glory. Then dad recounted the story of Gideon from the Book of Judges in the Bible.

Gideon was a wheat farmer whom God called to deliver the Israelites from the Midianites, who were oppressing them. With only 300 men, Gideon surrounded the enemy army at night. Gideon's men, armed only with torches and trumpets, were hardly a match for the massed forces in the valley below. But at Gideon's signal, 300 torches were bared, 300 trumpets blasted, and then 300 voices shouted, "The sword of the Lord and of Gideon!" The sleeping Midianites awoke terrified. Seeing themselves surrounded by torches, they imagined they were being attacked by a huge army. In the darkness and confusion, they attacked one another before turning to flee out of the country.

Dad pointed out that if God could use trumpets and torches, he could probably use skis. And a wheat farmer named James Mark could, with some help from the sword of the Lord, serve God in a mighty way as a ski racer.

Afterwards dad and I knelt at the kitchen table to commission me as a missionary—a missionary on skis. No one mentioned it, but in the back of my mind was the memory of the commitment I had made to be a missionary when I was eight. Christ was to be number one, and skiing was to be my means of serving.

Later on, we saw another biblical parallel. Just as God often changed the names of men in the Bible when he appointed them to serve him—Abram became Abraham, Jacob became Israel, Gideon became Jerubbaal, Saul became Paul—so had I changed my name from Mark to Jim when I first started skiing competitively. It seemed like everything was pointing me to a career as God's skier.

From that night on, "The Sword of the Lord, and

the Skis of James Mark" became my motto. I had been inspired to ski fast before—the Nancy Greene movies and the desire to win and be noticed had seen to that—but now skiing took on a spiritual dimension. I had a holy calling. I was convinced that I was destined to win. I had to. If I was skiing for God, then I needed to win so he could be honored by my victories, and I would be respected when I told others about my beliefs.

The truth was, of course, that God wanted control of my skiing in order to mature me as a person—whether I won or not. But that night in the kitchen, I couldn't see that. In my teenage mind, God was now going to take over and bring success.

I thought that dedicating my skiing to God would take the pressure off, but it did just the opposite. In a strange twist, turning my racing into my mission made the competition take on eternal dimensions. Losing became not just a disappointment, but a disgrace to God.

For me skiing was no longer a sport—it was holy war.

Ten
UNDIVIDED GALL

NO ONE HAS EVER ACCUSED ME of being shy, and as I returned home from Kokanee Glacier, I was convinced that confidence and boldness were key ingredients in the success formula. I figured that to win, I had to be bold, especially now that I was God's representative on skis.

When I got home at the end of that summer, I told my parents, "I'm going to be on the national team by next spring."

"Don't get your hopes up too high," mom cautioned. "You've only been skiing for three years."

"I don't care. I'm gonna do it."

Some people might have considered my attitude brash, but I figured it wasn't brash if I lived up to it. I was reminded of a couple of earlier occasions when I'd stuck my neck out to make predictions. Once was when I'd gone to see a World Cup race for the first time.

Rossland, British Columbia, was on the World

Cup circuit in the spring of 1968. The World Cup competition had begun in the winter of 1966-67, so this was only its second year of existence. Nancy Greene and Jean-Claude Killy had won the World Cup the year before, and this year, as I faithfully kept track of the results in the papers, I knew that Nancy and Jean-Claude were on their way to doing it again.

I hitched a ride with Wayne Colborne for the 450-mile trip from Calgary to Rossland. Wayne was four years older than I, and he drove his family's camper. On the way we talked about what we would do when we got there.

I wanted to see Nancy Greene in person. After watching her films so many times, I felt I almost knew her. She was still the racer whose style I was trying to imitate. But I wanted to do more than mere spectating.

"I'm going to be a forerunner," I told Wayne.

"Fat chance," he said. "I'm sure they're already picked."

"They can always use one more," I said, more to convince myself than Wayne.

Forerunners are used at all major races to ski through the course just before the race to make sure the course is clear and to take off the light snow that has accumulated overnight. They are usually chosen from among the young racers in the area, but I wasn't going to let the fact that I was from Calgary keep me out.

As soon as Wayne and I arrived at Rossland, I started looking for Mickey Johnson, the coach of the British Columbia provincial ski team and the coordinator of the race.

I asked him if I could be a forerunner. He said all the forerunners had already been selected, but I kept pestering him.

"You can always add one more," I pleaded. I hounded him until he said, "Well, we'll see."

That was enough progress for the first day, I figured. Every time I saw him around the lodge or on the slopes during the practice days, I made a point of asking when I was supposed to be a forerunner.

Naturally, I'd brought my skis, and I spent the whole day on the slope chasing the action. Every time I saw Nancy Greene or Jean-Claude Killy, I followed them. Once they were climbing up the hill together, and I was right behind them, almost stepping on their skis.

The next day were the first races. Early in the morning, I was up and looking for Mickey Johnson. It was a long shot, but I knew the only chance I had was to make such a pest of myself that he had to say yes to get me out of his hair. I found him hurrying out of the lodge.

"Where do you need another forerunner? I'm ready to go."

"Oh, all right, Hunter. You can be the number three forerunner for the slalom race."

I grinned. I knew I had won. I was going to deliver the best forerun the World Cup had ever seen.

Forerunners have to be careful not to ski too hard

on their edges. If they do, they'll tear up the course. The other thing they have to keep in mind is skiing a good route, close to the poles, so you can clear the skiff of snow off the path the racers will be taking. And, of course, to fall and mar the course is an unforgivable sin.

Concentrating hard, I made my run after the other two forerunners. Mickey Johnson was waiting at the bottom.

"Good job, Hunter," he said. "We'll use you again."

So for every race after that, I got to be a forerunner. Wayne Colborne couldn't believe my gall. But, as I told him on the ride home, "If you want something, you have to go out and take it. No one is going to give it to you."

My second brash prediction didn't turn out quite as well. It was a couple of months after I'd successfully wangled the forerunner job at Rossland, and the skiing season was over. I'd placed third in the Alberta Junior C championships, and the Skimeister coaches had voted me most outstanding Skimeister. Nancy Greene, my inspiration and idol, came to the awards banquet to speak and present the trophies. It was one of my proudest moments.

Perhaps what happened afterwards could be excused on the grounds that I was carried away by the thrill of the award. But to be honest, I'd probably have done it regardless. I was just that kind of person.

Mom, dad, and I were sitting in the car waiting

for the parking lot to clear. Nancy Greene came out of the banquet room and walked toward her car. I stuck my head out the back window and yelled, "Hey, Nancy!"

She glanced up, saw me, and walked over.

"Congratulations on your award, Jim," she said.

I looked her in the eye and said evenly, "Nancy, someday I'll be better than you, and I'm going to win more medals than you have."

Immediately I was whapped on the back of the head by a well-placed blow from mom's hand. Nancy just smiled and pretended not to notice.

"Well, Jim," she said, "if you do that, it will be quite an accomplishment, something you can be proud of."

I was sure I could.

After placing third in the Junior C championships and winning the Most Outstanding Skimeister trophy, the next step should have been to make the Alberta team. But Guy Christie, the Alberta coach, said he didn't think I was good enough.

It was a major disappointment, but here, for once, the bottomless well of self-confidence proved an asset. I refused to believe that Guy Christie's rejection was valid. It simply wasn't possible that I wasn't good enough, I reasoned. After all, skiing was my mission. When skiing is an eternal issue, I simply couldn't allow a man's judgment to sabotage what I considered a divine master plan.

I did two things: I increased my training routine, and I wrote a letter to Al Raine, the alpine director of the Canadian Ski Association, informing him that I was good enough for the national team. If I couldn't be on the provincial team, I decided to skip it and go a step higher.

I'd always worked hard in training, but now I felt guilty any time I was not working out. Both dad and God were monitoring my progress. To relax was to waste time that should be applied to improving my conditioning or technique.

I was running ten miles each morning, doing eighty one-armed push-ups every day, lifting weights, and riding distances on my bicycle. About this time, I discovered I could hang from a door by my toes. It wasn't a stunt—it was a great way to strengthen the toes and the lower leg, so I added it to my training routine.

Someone asked Skimeister coach Ken Marchand if he thought I was training too much. "There's no such thing as overtraining," he said. "If a person can't relax, you shouldn't force him to. Jim is compensating for his life-style. Instead of partying and chasing girls like the other racers, Jim burns off that excess energy by extra work."

Ken encouraged me to keep training, even during the racing season. He was perceptive enough to see that I enjoyed working out—for me it was a form of recreation.

Since I'd seen that conditioning was so important in skiing, and since I was training more than any of the other skiers I knew, I felt I had some basis to be confident that I'd make the national team.

When I got Al Raine's reply to my letter, however, it wasn't encouraging. He was impressed with my confidence, but wanted some evidence of my ability. He asked for my race results.

I didn't have any to speak of. I hadn't won a race since my first Skimeister outing over three years ago. So I wrote Al a return letter simply repeating that I was good enough.

Al's second letter wasn't encouraging either, but he did offer me a glimmer of hope. He said he'd have to see if I was in shape to ski on the national level, and he arranged to meet me when he visited the University of Calgary a few weeks later.

Wayne Colborne and I both had hopes of making the national team, so we went together to the university. Al was in the athletic building, dressed in his running clothes. Immediately Wayne and I changed into our gym suits and met Al outside to go running.

The three of us started jogging along the roads around the university. After about fifteen minutes, Wayne and I noticed that Al had slowed down, but we kept going to show him we were in shape. Five minutes later, we'd lost him completely, but we figured he had stopped at the top of the hill and was watching us. So Wayne and I continued to run for almost an hour before Wayne suddenly pulled up short. He was looking up the hill.

"He's not up there," he said. "We might as well go back."

So we turned around and jogged back to the dressing room. Al was sitting on the bench, tenderly probing the blisters on his feet. He'd already taken a shower and must have returned to the dressing room immediately after we'd first lost him.

He looked up at Wayne and me.

"Well, I guess you're in shape," he said. "Now we'll have to see if you know how to ski. Let me know when there's enough snow this fall, and we'll go skiing at Sunshine."

As soon as the first snow fell that year, I gave Al a call.

"The snow's here. We're ready to go skiing."

So Al came back to Calgary the first week Sunshine opened. Dad was almost as excited as I was. He bought me a brand-new pair of Rossignol skis to show Al Raine how serious we were about my making the team. I followed Al all morning as he took me over the toughest slopes Sunshine had to offer, and I managed to keep up with him.

As a result, a few weeks later, I was invited to train with the national team at Lake Louise.

That training session was my opportunity to show what I could do. After a couple days of downhill training, the national team staged a race. The twenty national team candidates competed, and I finished eleventh. I felt I'd proved myself. I'd beaten nine national-level skiers, even if ten others had beaten me. At least I was competitive.

After that race, Wayne Colborne, Steve Becker, and I were selected to the *les espoir* (young hopefuls), just a step below the national team and a preliminary to international competition. My long shot had paid off. My boldness had gotten me that all-important invitation, but it also branded me. At our training camp at West Castle Mountain in Lethbridge, the other racers had all heard the story of how a presumptuous fifteen-year-old had pushed his way into the training camp. They gave me a hard time about it, and unfortunately, I couldn't really prove myself on skis—the weather was so windy and snowy that we couldn't race. We merely trained and trained and trained.

I raced that season in the Pontiac Cup races, a series of seven events for skiers just below national-team caliber. I never won a race, but finished consistently in the top five.

My reputation as a stunt man was also spreading. At each stop on the circuit, it became the thing to do to find the biggest jump and see if Hunter would take it. He always would. Bob Fugere, the *les espoir* coach, told a newspaper reporter that "Jim Hunter will be the greatest skier Canada's ever had if he doesn't kill himself first."

Brashness, I was convinced, was a quality required of champions, and it had a curious side effect—it succeeded in putting you in the spotlight, but it didn't keep you there long. I continually had to keep proving myself by doing more and more bizarre things—jumping over huge rocks, leaping off cornices, or sliding down a slope in my boots, without skis. I thrived on being put on the spot. I felt that being a champion boiled down to a simple issue—either you can do what you say you can do, or you can't. If you can, prove it. If you can't, shut up and get out. Since I never shut up, I constantly had to prove myself.

Unfortunately, I wasn't proving myself in competition, at least not to my satisfaction. I finished the season fourth in Pontiac Cup competition, not a bad finish, but I hadn't finished first in a race all year. It seemed that I was a great stunt man, but I began to wonder if I'd ever be a winner.

A vague feeling of doubt began to creep in—maybe I wasn't the skier I thought I was. I evaluated my approach to skiing and concluded that I wasn't as bold as I should be. My boldness had helped me to national competition, but it wasn't quite enough yet to let me win. I was developing a bad habit of just trying to finish the races standing up. By concentrating on avoiding falls, you finish consistently near the top, but never as number one. I vowed to myself that from now on, I'd go all out to win, even if a fall or two would disqualify me occasionally.

That spring, the national team officials invited me to join the team in Europe the next year and prepare for World Cup competition. I was sixteen years old, and my goal had been reached within the time I'd set for myself.

It was an unlikely route that I took to reach that goal—not starting to ski until I was twelve, not winning a single race after my first one as a Skimeister, and never making the provincial team—yet somehow I found myself a part of the Canadian national team. It was time to set another goal.

I told myself that I'd be in the Olympics when I was eighteen.

Eleven
WORLD CUP FEVER

AFTER MAKING THE NATIONAL TEAM, I thought only of the glamour of the European circuit. I considered myself under a lot of pressure to win, but I wasn't—at least not compared to what would come later.

I was sixteen years old, and had completed only grade eleven. Other parents might have refused to let their son pass up his last year of school to go to Europe and ski with the national team. But mom and dad said, "Jim, if you have the talent and you want to go, we'll let you, because God has given you the talent, and you should use it." All of the training and all the summer camps had been pointing to this, and now it was time to start seeing some results.

My first year was spent racing on the B team circuit—mostly biding my time. But I frequently pestered Al Raine and Coach Gilbert Mollard to give me a chance to make the A squad. At the Val d'Isere downhill in 1969, they did. They told me that if I was within six seconds of the winner, I'd stay on the A squad. Six seconds! That wouldn't be any problem, because I was going to win, or so I thought. But reality is a harsh teacher. I finished a humiliating twelve seconds behind.

Yet despite my impatience, I realized that no one expected me to walk away with the World Cup immediately. I was still young, still the kid with great potential. But I began to sense that the time was soon coming when I'd have to win, and the pressure would be severe.

George Duffield, the well-known sportscaster for the CBC, wrote me a handwritten letter just before Christmas of 1969. He said:

Dear Jim,

I was really pleased to see that you got into the downhill at Val d'Isere. No doubt you were the most surprised of all. Although your debut was, to say the least, less than spectacular, I hope you realize that great things don't always happen overnight. The main thing to remember is to always get in the gate to win, at *all* costs. . . . Some of the others have been around so long and hearing the old phrase "Get in the first fifteen" that they fall short and always will. Don't you get caught in that malaise. When you win, you are in the first fifteen. There's no room on the future national team for anyone who doesn't have the overwhelming desire to win.

Right now the team needs a leader it can respect. That means someone who wins races. That leader could be you if you work hard enough. You've got the desire, and you've got the ability, but you have to (naturally) improve your technique. I don't think I'm telling you anything you haven't already been told by Gilbert. All the old cliches are true, Jim. Nice guys finish last. . . . The Canadians are the most popular national team on the circuit. Why? Because they're no threat to anyone's position in the finish list. Now's the time to stop being a "nice guy."

Maintain your desire and drive and you *will be the next Canadian World Champion.* . . . I believe you can be there if you want to. The best part is, if you make the move and win some races, you'll have other Canadians in charging up your back wanting to take your place. Then and only then will we be a force to be reckoned with in skiing. Remember, it's only two years to Sapporo. Canada could have an Olympic champion in two consecutive Olympic games. . . .

Best regards,
George Duffield

A year later, during my second year in Europe, a major upheaval shook the Canadian national team and plopped that dreaded pressure squarely on me earlier than I expected, and just a year before the 1972 Olympics.

For several years, the Canadian team had been a veteran team. It was full of "old guys"—twenty-four and twenty-five years old. Peter Duncan, Jerry Rinaldi, Keith Shepherd, and Bert and Dan Irwin had been on the team for almost ten years. In 1970-71, some younger skiers, such as Reto Barrington, Derek Robbins, Mike Culver, and myself, had come along to seriously challenge the older guys.

Coach Mollard said that the A squad members would be chosen at our summer camp in Kaprun, Austria, solely on the basis of time trials—four slalom races and four giant slaloms. The older guys didn't like the arrangement.

"Why should we go all out at training camp?" they argued. "We don't need to be up now. We need to save it for the season."

Mollard was tough. He wouldn't put up with that, and didn't change his mind. A lot of dissension was aroused. Mollard insisted on everyone skiing all day and then going through a tough physical training routine in the evening. All this was fine with me—I would have done the work anyway whether Mollard had ordered it or not—but I could see the older guys' point. They'd been racing so many years, it was hard to maintain peak intensity too long.

Nevertheless, Mollard staged the time trials. As it turned out, I won all four giant slalom runs and came in second in three of the four slaloms. I finished first overall, and Reto Barrington was second.

Mollard began riding the older guys more and more. Eventually midway through the season, he and the other national team officials made a decision, a tough one, to go with the younger skiers. We weren't doing too well in World Cup competition anyway, the older skiers weren't getting along with Mollard, and the team officials were thinking ahead to next year's Olympics at Sapporo, Japan.

Suddenly most of the older guys were let go, and

only three racers remained from the last year's squad. It's questionable whether or not it was the right decision. To Canadians, "old" is twenty-four or twenty-five. To Europeans, you're not old until you're thirty. Add to that the fact that Canadians usually don't start skiing as early as Europeans, and that we have to adjust to their culture to compete. It means that experience is more important than the Canadian officials were willing to admit.

With the leadership and experience gone, the burden fell on young skiers in their first year of World Cup competition. On European teams, when younger racers beat out older racers, they keep the older guys around to teach the newer ones. I remember Austrians David Zwilling, Reinhard Tritscher, and Karl Schranz still hanging around with their team long after they'd stopped racing. They were helping the young Austrians—Franz Klammer, Werner Grissmann, and Anton Steiner—by teaching them the subtleties of technique and the idiosyncrasies of the different courses. The Canadian officials said they couldn't afford financially to keep the other guys around, but it cost the team the maturity the veterans could have provided.

I felt a new responsibility had been given to me, and I reacted to the pressure the only way I knew how—by working out even harder. Even the day before a race, I'd be up at 6:00 A.M. to go run two miles, do fifty push-ups, a hundred sit-ups, and a hundred rope skips. After the race and after supper, I'd repeat the workout. I couldn't figure out why I seemed to be tired all the time. My legs seemed dead during the races, so I tried increasing my distance running, but the extra conditioning didn't solve the problem. I was still tired.

Eventually, I got so run-down that when I returned to Canada for a break, I went to our family doctor. Dr. Still told me that I was working too hard. He said I needed a rest. I didn't believe him.

By failing to prepare, you're preparing to fail was the motto I often repeated to myself. I was convinced that there was no such thing as too much work. I'd always been taught that if you work more than anyone else, it will eventually pay off. I wasn't ready to abandon that philosophy yet. I lived with a continual sense of unpreparedness—there was always something more I could, and really should, be doing. After each race, I went through a list of "if onlys"—if only I'd run farther, if only I'd studied the course more, if only I'd done more push-ups, then I would have won.

But during the week I was home, I followed the doctor's advice and didn't work out. I rejoined the World Cup circuit in Heavenly Valley, California. It was a steep, icy course—just my style—but I wasn't sure of myself because I hadn't been working out regularly. I figured I was out of shape.

Strangely enough, the Heavenly Valley giant slalom was the best race I'd ever run. After the first run, Gustavo Thoeni of Italy was leading and I was well back in the standings. But in the second run, despite being in the second seed and starting after the course was already well chewed by previous skiers, I turned in the second-best time. It was good enough to move me into ninth place for the event, earning me two World Cup points. They were the first World Cup points I'd ever earned, and this was easily the highlight of the year.

Even winning the giant slalom event a few weeks later in the Can-Am championships at Whistler Mountain, British Columbia, wasn't as big a thrill. But I didn't make the connection between my week's rest and my good performance. It wasn't until a couple of years later when I met Jean-Claude Killy that I realized there might be a connection. Jean-Claude said, "Energy is the key to racing."

He pointed out that he never trains for two days prior to any competition. He allows his body to recover its strength so he can go full bore during the race. But I was slow to accept this, even when it came from Jean-Claude. After the Heavenly Valley race, I immediately started up my full-scale training regimen again.

Winning the World Cup points at Heavenly Valley and winning the giant slalom at Whistler Mountain did make me realize one thing, however—I was heir apparent to lead the Canadian national team. At the beginning of the 1970-71 season, I was a B squad racer trying to make the A team. At the end of the season, I was not only on the A team, but I was Canada's best hope to win World Cup points and an Olympic medal next year.

I felt more pressure than ever, and again I reacted the only way I knew how: more training. Back on the farm in Shaunavon, dad and I devised a whole conditioning program tailored to the farm setting.

Each morning, I continued to do my push-ups, rope skipping, and running—now up to ten miles some days. I practiced slalom technique by setting up a series of old tires and jumping side to side from one to the next. If I touched the tires with either of my feet, I made myself do fifty push-ups. In addition, while I was driving the tractor, I discovered ways to train from behind the wheel. I did my sit-ups on the seat of the tractor as I drove. After that I stood on the seat and practiced my prejumps—tucked in a racing crouch, I'd leap as high as I could, bring my knees up to my chest, and return to the tractor seat in my tuck. I'd do that as many times as I could before the tractor needed a steering correction.

Sometime during the middle of the summer, I read a magazine article explaining how astronauts were spun around in sophisticated modules to train them to keep their balance in a weightless environment. I mentioned it to dad, and it inspired another of his brainstorms. We didn't have sophisticated equipment, but we did have a huge tractor with wheels large enough to crawl into, and if being spun around could give astronauts a better sense of balance, why shouldn't it work for skiers?

So we gathered a couple of old pillows and wedged me inside the rim of the tractor tire, while dad got in the cab. He drove around in tight circles for two or three minutes. I had my head between my knees, so I didn't see much while dad was driving. When the tractor stopped, I crawled out and tried to get into a racing crouch. The world kept spinning, and I couldn't keep up with it. I tumbled over. My body refused to remain upright.

Dad said, "That just shows that you need to work on it." So we kept trying it, and sure enough, before the week was over, I was able to crawl out of the wheel and stagger into a crouch without toppling over. After that, it was sort of fun, and I was sure it would help my skiing.

I kept extensive notes on everything I could think of—what I ate, my pulse rate, the hours I slept, the miles I ran, the exercises I did, and the various wax combinations that work best on different kinds of snow. I drew diagrams of the various World Cup courses and how to get down them the quickest. I was also reading the Bible daily and taking notes on what I thought about it. Most of those journal entries repeated my determination to win so that God would be honored.

The next year would be my first full year with the A team, and it was an Olympic year besides. I knew it was time to be more than a kid with great potential; it was time to be great.

Twelve
ON SCHEDULE IN SAPPORO

SAPPORO IS A CROWDED CITY on Hokkaido, the northernmost island of Japan. When the Canadian ski team arrived, the streets were choked with cars, buses, and pedestrians. It seemed that the entire world was trying to jam into one city for the 1972 Winter Olympics. It took us over an hour for our little Japanese bus to creep its way to the Olympic village.

After we arrived and the necessary paperwork was done for credentials and room assignments, the first place I headed was the cafeteria. I'd heard stories about the food provided for Olympic athletes, and I wasn't disappointed. In the Olympic village, there were actually four different international dining rooms, and they were all free for the athletes. I managed to try all four throughout the course of the week, but mostly I lived on steaks, Coke, and Orange Crush.

The big issue that year was Karl Schranz and the

International Olympic Committee's charges of professionalism. Just prior to the Olympics, IOC President Avery Brundage threatened to disqualify about forty skiers for earning money on the circuit. Most of the European nations said that if their skiers were barred, their teams would withdraw. Four days before the games began, Brundage disqualified only Karl Schranz—and the games went on.

To be perfectly honest, I was so wrapped up in the excitement of merely being there that I didn't pay much attention to the controversy. I knew I was an amateur, and that was all that mattered to me. Naturally, I would have liked to see Schranz ski. To me, he was like a pillar of iron—an incredibly strong person, both mentally and physically. I'd heard stories about how he trained—riding his bike down the Arlberg Pass, back up the pass, down the other side, and back up again—120 miles in one day. I was awed. Schranz was the one person on the World Cup circuit that I never had the courage to communicate with—all the other top racers, such as Bernhard Russi, Patrick Russel, Gustavo Thoeni, and Franz Klammer, I felt free to joke around with, but Schranz was different. He was one of a kind.

I was sorry when Schranz was eventually banned from the competition. But it gave me a glimmer of hope—maybe I could win the downhill. That was the event I figured I had the best chance in.

The opening ceremony was, for me, an emotional experience. Despite the controversy about professionalism and the Austrian team's threat to pull out of the competition, I was struck by the remarkable quality that sports had to bring people together. Athletic competition was truly a worldwide phenomenon. As the Canadian team paraded through the streets of Sapporo and into the Olympic Stadium, I felt a part of a long and noble tradition.

Thousands of people lined the route to the stadium to watch the procession of athletes, and we knew millions more were watching on television. I thought back to the plane ride from Europe to Japan. Before refueling in Athens, the plane had circled the ancient Greek Olympic site. I was humbled and near tears of joy to be able to compete in the continuation of those games.

It was something I'd always dreamed of. At twelve, I'd set a goal to ski for the Canadian team. At sixteen, I had reset my goal to be in the Olympics. And now at eighteen, I was there.

The excitement was contagious. Looking around at the athletes from all the other countries, I could see they were as inspired as I was. I saw athletes I'd heard of but never met—Canadian skater Karen Magnusson and hockey players Mark and Marty Howe, and from a distance, American skater Janet Lynn.

We marched past the stand where the emperor of Japan and Avery Brundage sat. We doffed our hoods in salute and marched on to take our places inside the speed skating rink. Then the torchbearer came running in to light the Olympic flame. Thousands of balloons were released to drift into the sky, and my emotions were almost as high. I was ready to do anything to win a gold medal.

After the opening ceremonies, we had five days until the first men's skiing event, the downhill.

The site of the downhill was forty miles from Sapporo, and because of the traffic, it was almost a four-hour trip. For our days of training, we had to leave very early in the morning to get there in time to do any serious work.

Only three Canadian male skiers had qualified for the Olympics—Reto Barrington, Derek Robbins, and me. The three of us were accompanied by three coaches. The Austrians, by contrast, had five skiers and seventeen officials.

As we trained on the Olympic downhill course, I discovered that except for one thing, it was my kind of run. The entire course was hard and fast—perfect for me—but the first part of the run was a series of back-and-forth turns. I still hadn't learned to turn as well as I should have—I was digging in my edges too deeply and slowing myself down.

After the turns came a relatively straight part of the course where the Japanese had built some bumps to make it harder. Then came the final pitch that was very steep, very straight, and very much my favorite part of the course.

By the day of the race, I had convinced myself that I had a chance for a medal. I woke up that morning with the worst case of nerves I'd ever had. I thought I was going to be sick and miss the race. I was thinking more about the medal than about the course and what I had to do. I wanted so badly to win, and I knew that the downhill would probably be my only chance of doing so.

When we got to the mountain, I still wasn't feeling well, but the Japanese ski coaches unwittingly provided a partial cure with what I considered comic relief. As the Japanese skiers were waiting to start, the coaches would come up behind and smack them hard on the back of the head and yell at them in Japanese, trying to get them psyched up. It was their way of attempting to get the skiers inspired to push themselves down the hill. I couldn't help laughing.

So I was feeling better as I took my place in the starting gate. Switzerland's Bernhard Russi was going to be the one to beat. He'd done well all during the World Cup season, and as he'd made his run earlier, I noticed he was turning very well. With Schranz out of the picture, Russi was the favorite, and his time of 1:51.43 was the best so far.

When my turn came, well back in the starting order, I was still thinking about a medal. I blasted out of the start and rushed into the turns. As I leaned into the first turn, I knew I was off to a great start. The second and third turns were also smooth, but on four and five, I allowed my edges to bite a little deeply, and I felt myself lose momentum.

By then, however, I was out of the turns and into the bumps. This was my part of the run, and I had to make up for the time I'd lost on the turns. I scooted through the bumps and came to the final pitch, tucked into a tight crouch. It was so steep and fast that the crowd lining the course rushed by in a blur. I loved it—I could feel myself making up time. I rocketed through the finish, and I was sure I had won.

I skidded to a stop and turned around to look at the big timing clock off to the side of the course. It was a cruel shock when the clock flashed 1:55.16. I hadn't won; in fact, I wasn't even in the running for a medal. My time was good for only twentieth place. I couldn't believe I was that far back. Even though twentieth was the best finish a Canadian male had ever made in Olympic competition, I felt I had let down my team, my country, and God.

There had been several articles in newspapers that year both in Europe and in Canada reporting that "Jim Hunter skis for God." I'd never hidden my faith, but now that it was being publicized, I felt it was an absolute necessity for me to win. I had often prayed, "Lord, if you want people to listen to me when I tell them about you, you've got to make me a winner." But something had gone wrong.

We left the ski area at two o'clock and didn't get back to Sapporo until six-thirty. It was one of the most miserable 4½-hour bus rides I've ever taken. Two years earlier, when I was on the Canadian B team, I had been told I was too young to race in the 1970 World Championships. I'd told myself that I could have won those if I'd been given the chance. Now at Sapporo I'd had that chance, and I hadn't come close to winning. To me, twentieth was worthless.

There were two more events, however, and only by consciously turning my thoughts to them was I able to get over the downhill disappointment.

The next day was the women's giant slalom, and chubby little Marie-Therese Nadig of Switzerland upset Annemarie Proell of Austria, just as she had two days earlier in the downhill. I was encouraged that a relative unknown could come from nowhere to beat the favorite not once, but twice. Besides that, Laurie Kreiner from Canada placed fourth in the giant slalom. Slowly I convinced myself that if they could do it, I could.

While the women's giant slalom was going on, Reto, Derek, the coaches, and I went to look at the men's giant slalom run. When we got there, we saw something very unusual, but something that gave me another bit of hope. It had snowed the night before, and the course was covered with several inches of new snow. But swarming all over the giant slalom run was the Japanese army, clearing the fresh snow from the run and exposing the harder, icy snow underneath that they had watered the day before. It was comical to watch these men without skis trying to keep their balance on the steep slope. Occasionally one man would fall and start sliding down the mountain. There were so many soldiers on the hill that he would slide into two or three others, knocking them off their feet. It would start a chain reaction, a bowling-alley effect. The Japanese soldiers were laughing as much as we were.

"Look at what they're doing," I shouted at Reto.

"This is going to be just like Heavenly Valley last year."

I started to get excited. Heavenly Valley had been hard when I finished ninth and won my first World Cup points. Now this run was going to be good and icy. Things were starting to go my way.

Eric Haker of Norway was the favorite to win the giant slalom, and after the first day of competition, sure enough, he had turned the best time. But the course was so fast that no one was going to be able to run away from the rest of the field. All the times were fairly close. Haker was followed by Alfred Hagn of Germany and Italy's Gustavo Thoeni. I wound up thirteenth after the first run, and I was happy with my position and looking forward to the second run the next day. With any sort of luck at all, I figured I ought to be able to get into the top ten in the second run. I set that as my goal.

The next day, I felt good. I didn't feel the pressure to win that I had in the downhill. The giant slalom wasn't my specialty, even though I usually managed to do fairly well in it. Ever since Skimeisters, I'd considered myself a downhiller, and that's where I felt the pressure to succeed.

Waiting is the trademark of a ski racer's life. You have to wait for hours to make a two-minute run. And as I sat in the shelter at the top of the giant slalom course, waiting for my turn to ski over to the start, I watched the first racers make their runs on television. Everyone crowded around as Haker made his run. I could tell the course was just as fast as yesterday, and Haker was really moving. Halfway through the run, he was six-tenths of a second ahead. But then something happened. Haker lost his balance, his skis slipped out from under him, he fell and went sliding off the course.

Someone groaned, and we all watched silently to see if he was all right. He slowly got to his feet unhurt, but I'll never forget his disappointment as he sideslipped the rest of the way down the course, disqualified from the race.

Alfred Hagn was then in the best position to win. Hagn, like me, had never won on the circuit, and now was his big chance. Perhaps it was the pressure, or perhaps yesterday's second-place finish was a fluke. I don't know. But whatever the reason, Hagn skied badly. He finished standing up, but we doubted his time would win him the gold. The next racer, Gustavo Thoeni, made sure of it. Gustavo just seemed to have the rhythm, making the turns effortlessly. He easily beat Hagn's time.

I couldn't watch any more on TV. It was time to head down to the start. I was ready.

There were two parts to this run—the pitch, and the flats. The turns were made up on the pitch, and then the course flattened out at the bottom. Yesterday, I'd done well on the turns, but I'd lost time on the flats just before the finish. Today I wasn't going to let that happen.

As soon as I left the start, I knew this was going to be a good run. It was as if I was detached, another person watching myself ski. Through the turns everything went perfect—my edges were biting just deep enough for control, but not so much to slow me down. I shot down the pitch and entered the flats knowing I had a good chance to crack the top ten. On the flats, I knew I was safe—I couldn't catch a tip and fall now, so I just started blasting—skating and poling hard—trying to shave every possible hundredth of a second off my time.

I finished with the seventh-best second-run time and thought I had a good chance to sneak into the top ten for the event. But Alain Penz and Andrzej Bachleda-Curus tied for ninth place just ahead of me, dropping me to eleventh. It didn't bother me, though. I was so pleased with my second run. Doing that well in the giant slalom was an unexpected thrill. It made up for the downhill disaster.

Only one event remained—the slalom. I've never been very good at the slalom. Someone once described it as "a controlled fall down an icy hill." It's a race for specialists—a short, quick event—a sprint. It's a completely different discipline from downhill and giant slalom—it's hard to be good in all three. Slalom skis are generally taller, slimmer, and more flexible, to enable the racer to make sixty turns in one minute. Turns were never my strength.

I knew I didn't have a chance of winning. I was nervous, but only because I was scared of embarrassing myself. My goal was just to get down the hill standing up.

Jean-Noël Augert of France was everyone's pick to win. But on a practice run the day before, someone had forgotten to remove the steel rod used to make holes in the snow for the slalom poles. Instead of a bamboo slalom pole at the end of the run, this five-foot steel rod was jammed into the snow. Augert flashed down the run, hitting his hips on the poles as he went by, as all slalom racers are supposed to do to keep their turns as tight as possible. The bamboo is flexible and gives when the skier's hip hits it. But when Augert smacked the steel rod, it didn't give, and Augert was knocked off his skis and bruised his hip.

I think it affected his skiing during the event the next two days. He finished fifth behind Spain's surprising Fernando Francisco Ochoa, Italy's Gustavo Thoeni and his cousin Rolano Thoeni, and Henri Duvillard of France. I finished twenty-first and was pleased that I hadn't humiliated myself by falling.

The Olympics was over for me. I just hung around the next few days until the closing ceremony. I hadn't won a medal, but I was enjoying myself exploring the Olympic village and sightseeing around the area.

In the closing ceremony, I got the surprise of my life. The medals were awarded for figure skating, hockey, and the men's slalom. Then they announced the results for the combined alpine events. Gustavo Thoeni was first, Walter Tresch was second, and Jim Hunter was third! I had no idea I was even close. And Reto Barrington finished fourth.

The award had something of an asterisk attached because the combined medal wasn't awarded by the International Olympic Committee, but by the

FIS—it was an FIS medal for Olympic competition. It was determined by the FIS points earned in each of the three events, based on how many seconds a racer finished behind the winner. About twelve racers had raced in all three events, thus qualifying for the combined medal.

But all of this was mere technicality as far as I was concerned. It didn't matter. I had won a bronze medal in Olympic competition. For an eighteen year old, I figured this was a good start. Now, at last, I was on my way. My formula was working.

Thirteen
NOT IN THE SCRIPT

IN YEARS PAST, the Canadian ski team had gone to Europe for the experience. Now, after the Olympics, we entered the World Cup competition looking for wins.

Until now, there had been a psychological barrier in Europe. The Europeans intimidated most of the Canadians and Americans. We were on their slopes, most of the ski equipment came from their countries, and they came from a long and near-religious tradition of ski racing . . . and winning. We were relative newcomers to the sport. No Canadian male had ever broken through the European domination of World Cup racing—we were still looking for our first win.

I refused to let myself be awed by the European skiers, and especially after the Olympic experience, I was ready to smash the psychological barrier and make a name for the Canadians. So far, my plan for success was on schedule. The next thing that was supposed to happen was for me to win a World Cup race this year.

At the first race of the 1972-73 season, in Val d'Isere, France, I almost pulled it off. In the giant slalom, despite being in the second seed and having to start after the fifteen skiers in the first seed had already hacked up the course, I made two strong runs. In the second, I almost fell, but I jammed my poles into the snow in front of my skis, regained my balance, and finished the race. I wound up with a fourth-place finish—the first time I'd ever been in the top five in any World Cup event, and the best finish ever for a Canadian male racer.

It marked my introduction to the fanatic European racing crowds. I was amazed how closely the Europeans followed ski racing. Huge crowds showed up at every race. And now, all of a sudden, it seemed that everyone on the streets recognized me. My autograph became worth seeking. At last, I thought, things were starting to go the way they were supposed to.

My smug self-satisfaction didn't last long. Gerard Rubaud, the racing director of Rossignol, who supplied me with my skis, came up to me right after the Val d'Isere race. I thought he was going to congratulate me. He did shake my hand and tell me I'd done pretty well, but in the same breath he said, "How come you didn't win?"

"Well, I tried," I said. "I made a mistake on the second run and almost fell. That's probably why I didn't win."

Gerard's left hand smacked me hard on the back of the head, just about knocking me over.

"Next time you win, okay?"

Then I realized that fourth place might look like the top of the world to a win-starved Canadian, but to those in racing, only first place was good enough. I had a ways to go.

What the fourth-place finish did, however, was establish me as a serious contender. I started to be invited to press conferences and receptions for World Cup racers. These affairs were mobbed with rabid racing fans, a stark contrast to the casual attitude toward racing in Canada.

At one of these receptions, just before the World Cup events began at Madonna di Campiglio, Italy, Patrick Lang introduced himself to me. He was a writer for the Swiss papers and the son of Serge Lang, the man who had helped start World Cup competition.

"I have this strange feeling, Jim," he said, "that you're going to win something very soon. In fact, I have a feeling that it's going to be this week."

I just nodded, but inside I was terribly excited. Could it be? Was this going to be the race where I'd get my first win? The timing was right—the next scene in my script called for a first-place finish. Maybe Madonna was the setting. I began to have the same "strange feeling" that Patrick Lang had mentioned.

The day before the race, all afternoon was set aside for course inspection. Since we had plenty of time, and largely for psych purposes, I decided to climb the course on my skis instead of taking the lift and sideslipping down as usual. Walking up a giant slalom course takes a long time—it's something over a mile and a half. I was so mentally up, though, that I didn't mind the climb. It was a great way to study the run.

At the bottom of the course, I noticed there wasn't enough snow. The Italian army had trucked in snow to cover the final pitch and sprayed water on it at night so it would freeze. Then just before daybreak, they added more snow on top. The whole mixture, however, was only about four inches deep, and I wondered how it would stand up to a whole day of racing.

The rest of the way up the course, I was bombarded with questions and comments from the European racers. They cracked jokes about Canadians not knowing that ski slopes ran downhill.

"Do you think that will help you win?" more than one passing racer asked with a cocky grin.

"We'll see" was all I said.

I finished my inspection, ignoring the snide comments from the Europeans.

The next morning I woke up about eight o'clock because Reto Barrington was leaving the room in his ski clothes.

"Where are you going?" I yawned.

"To an inspection."

"What inspection?" I asked. As far as I knew, the only thing on the schedule that day was the race at ten-thirty.

"Scotty told us last night that there would be an

inspection from eight-thirty to nine-thirty this morning."

"Why didn't he tell me?"

"I don't know," Reto said as he walked out the door.

I was irritated. This was Scott Henderson's first year as coach of the Canadian men's ski team. He had been a racer until he shattered a leg in a fall in 1969. I couldn't figure out why Scotty would tell Reto about this morning's inspection and ignore me. I rushed to put on my ski clothes, and stormed out to find an explanation.

Scott and his wife Sully were having breakfast in the restaurant on the first floor of the hotel. I marched into the restaurant with my ski boots on—something of a no-no in European resorts. I wasn't thinking about etiquette. I stomped over to the table.

"Scotty, what's the idea of not telling me there was an inspection this morning?"

"You don't need an inspection. You climbed the course yesterday."

"Listen, if there's an inspection, then I want to know about it. It's not for you to decide whether I need it or not. Let me make that decision."

I was getting mad. Looking back, I realize I went overboard—Scotty had told the team about the inspection the night before at supper, but I had, as usual, left the table early to check my skis. We had just missed connections. But at the moment, feeling the pressure of race day, I overreacted. I wanted Scotty to see that I was serious about this race. We couldn't be messing around.

"What am I supposed to do now?" I demanded. "The inspection starts in fifteen minutes, and I've got to get over there if I'm going to get the whole thing in, and I haven't even had breakfast. What am I going to eat?"

Just then the waiter came up with Scott's orange juice. I was so miffed, I took the orange juice and drank it in one gulp before walking out of the room.

I made the inspection run, this time working from top to bottom, and rode the lift back up to the top of the mountain. I then sat in the restaurant up there drinking tea, waiting for the race to begin.

After a while, Scott showed up. Neither of us said a thing about our earlier conversation. Together we went over to the start, where off to the side about eight practice gates had been set up. I took a warm-up run through the practice gates, and my timing was perfect. Everything seemed to come together. I remembered what Patrick Lang had said, and I had a hunch he was going to be right.

Scotty and I headed over to the start. It was almost time to go.

I noticed my goggles had some moisture on the inside lens. They were the new Carrera No-Wipe goggles that had just been introduced. You didn't have to wipe them to clear them—you only had to take them off, shake them, and let the air evaporate the moisture.

So I handed the goggles to Scotty and asked him to clear them while I positioned myself in the start. Apparently Scotty wasn't familiar with the new goggles—he took out a rag, and wiped the inside of the lenses, and handed them back to me. When I put them on, they were so scratched I couldn't even see the first gate.

"Oh, Scotty," I groaned. "I don't know why they hired you for this job. Give me your goggles."

I reached over and pulled the goggles off his head and put them on. Scotty finally lost control.

"Hunter, I've got news for you. You're not the only racer on the mountain this morning. I've only got a million other things to think about during a race, and believe it or not, not all of them are wrapped up around you."

Just then the starter said, "Ten seconds."

I couldn't think of a reply, so I just flipped the scratched goggles at Scotty, quickly adjusted the new ones, and poised myself to leap through the start.

"Five-four-three-two-one."

And I was off. I was so mad, almost uncontrollably mad, that I exploded out of the start. I don't think I touched the snow for ten feet. I skied with total abandonment. The next thing I knew, I was on the final pitch, taking the last six gates, doing everything with a quiet fury.

But I noticed something wasn't quite right. It took me a moment or two to realize what it was. It hit me as I passed the last gate and blasted toward the finish. It was the total silence. Usually the crowds lining the courses are yelling and screaming as the racer goes by. But they weren't now. Everyone was quiet. I couldn't figure out why.

I found out later that it was because my halfway time had just been announced over the P.A. I was a full second ahead of the leaders Gustavo Thoeni and David Zwilling. I hadn't heard it—I was just roaring down the hill.

As I blasted through the finish, I saw the German coach Harold Schonhar standing up in the middle of the finish area, his eyes glued to the scoreboard, and his fists tensed at ear level.

When my time was flashed on the big clock—1:56.02—Harold shot his hands above his head and jumped up and down, screaming, "You won! You won!"

I was still trying to slow down, and he was right in my way. I ran into him, but he wrapped his arms around me, and I came to an abrupt stop.

"You won! You won!" he kept yelling.

Then suddenly the crowd erupted. They'd been silent before, but when the time was flashed, all the spectators went crazy. A racer from the second seed, number twenty-eight, had come from way down the list to win the first run of the giant slalom. It was almost unheard of.

I was halfway to my goal. A strong second run that afternoon would give me that long-awaited World Cup win.

I made my way through the crowd to the hotel for some lunch, and then went to my room for a nap. I was exhausted from the emotion.

When I got up an hour later, I went downstairs to the ski room and saw assistant coach Bob Saunders working on my skis with a ten-inch single crosscut file. I always used a double crosscut file file on my skis. The file Saunders was using was making big nicks in the edges, just ruining my skis.

"Saunders," I said. "Don't touch those skis. I'll do it."

So I finished sharpening the edges as best I could, but there was still a couple of nicks I couldn't repair. Then I went back upstairs with my skis and found Scotty.

"Scotty, what did you let that idiot work on my skis for?"

"Why? What'd he do?"

"Look at what he did. He destroyed them."

"Don't worry about it," Scotty said. "Relax."

"Aw, Henderson," I moaned. "You and Saunders are really a pair. A couple of banana brains. They ought to send you back to Canada."

I just turned my back and walked out. Later, I discovered it was a set-up. Scotty had always been telling me I'd ski better if I'd just relax and forget about form and technique during the race. He'd seen me forget everything except my fury during the first run, and I'd skied the best race of my life. If that's what it took to make me ski with total abandon, Scotty wanted to do it again. He figured I might get suspicious if he provoked me again, so he had Saunders try. It worked. I was irate.

I headed out to go back up the mountain. I had plenty of time, but I wanted to walk off my irritation. On my way through town, I passed a little photo shop that had a big picture of me in the window. It had been taken on that morning's run, and already it was being sold. Again, I marveled at the difference in attitudes toward ski racing between Europeans and Canadians.

As I neared the lift, I saw Patrick Lang.

"See, I told you something great was going to happen," he said.

"I hope it happens in the second run."

"Why? Don't you think it will?"

"I'm convinced it will. Nothing's going to change."

He wished me luck, and as I turned to go up the mountain, I had a decision to make. I could take the lift and make an inspection run, or I could climb up the run again and hope I didn't get too tired. It didn't take long to decide.

I told myself that I was in good enough shape to climb it, and besides, I'd psyched out the opposition by climbing the first time. Maybe it would work again. So I started stepping up the hill.

Before I got too far, Eberardo Schmalz, an Italian racer, walked over to me.

"I guess if you win, we'll all have to start climbing the course, won't we?"

I grinned, but suddenly the impact of the situation hit me. I started to feel the pressure. I was just one good run away from winning a World Cup race. I could prove myself. It would make all worthwhile the snide comments I'd taken about my brashness, my life-style, and my religion. It would be the payoff for all those years of training. It would prove to me that the claims I'd been making about my ability weren't just idle boasting. And finally I'd get the recognition I thought was necessary to make my life more useful for God.

Hiking up the hill, however, was good therapy for the pressure. It gave me something to do to take my mind off the situation. By the time I got to the top of the run, the tension wasn't boiling over—it was just simmering on the back burner.

I would be starting the second run in the fifteenth spot. The first seed always goes first, and then the second seed goes in the order of their finish in the first run. One of the first-seed racers had fallen on the first run and was disqualified, so only fourteen racers were ahead of me.

When my turn came, I was still thinking about my skis. I wondered about the nicks in the edges and hoped they wouldn't make much of a difference.

I charged through the first half of the run smoothly. My halfway time left me six-tenths ahead. When I came to the final pitch and the last eight gates, I was a full second ahead of everybody.

That was the place where the snow had been trucked in by the army. By this time of the afternoon, it had started to melt, and some twigs and grass were protruding through the slush. Sparks started flying from where my metal edges hit rocks just below the surface.

Sweeping around the corner, I started down the pitch, made the first gate without any problem, turned around the second easily, and headed for number three.

I knew I was probably ahead, but I wasn't going

to slow down—this run was all-out to win.

As I skidded around the third turn, my legs got too far apart, my outside ski slipped, and I felt myself losing my balance. Frantically I dug in, but the rocks didn't allow my edges to catch. I was still on my feet and barely made it past the fourth gate.

But now I had to shift my weight to turn the other direction. It was steep, and my ski slipping caused me to slide too low. I tried to collect myself, but the skis let go again. My feet went out from under me, and I slid on my side past the next gate.

There was total silence. It was like the world had ended. I was out of the race. At that moment I didn't have any desire to ever ski again. I knew I'd had my chance to win, and I'd missed it.

The next week was Christmas break, and I went home. I tried to get mentally prepared for the second half of the season, but the job was still incomplete when we got to Wengen, Switzerland, a couple of weeks later.

By now, Europeans knew who Jungle Jim Hunter was, and he was getting his share of press coverage, but I was more obsessed with winning than ever. To come so close and go away empty-handed was devastating. If I had won at Madonna, I'm sure I would have immediately become a consistent winner. My racing success was largely determined by my mental state, and if I'd won, I'm sure it would have continued. As it was, I had to start all over.

But in the Wengen slalom, I caught a tip and fell. I hadn't checked the bindings carefully before the race, and snow was wedged between the boot and the ski, and as a result, the bindings didn't release and I severely pulled the ligaments and tendons in my ankle. I had to go home to Canada for physiotherapy.

While I was in Calgary for two months, recovering from the injury, I met a girl who was unlike almost any other I'd ever met. Her name was Gail Jespersen, and she wasn't at all interested in ski racing.

Gail attended First Alliance Church in Calgary, and had asked me to speak to the church's college and career young people one night when I was home for Christmas. I had worked up a presentation showing some comparisons between skiing and a life of faith in God. In both skiing and the Christian life, a person needs a goal, a line, and contact.

Goal: The only way a ski racer can win is if his only concern is getting to the bottom of the hill as fast as possible. Likewise, for a Christian to live a life that pleases God, that goal has to be foremost in the person's mind.

Line: On all courses, whether slalom, giant slalom, or downhill, you've got to have the right line. If you're four feet off that one turn on the downhill, you may be three seconds out at the bottom. In the Christian life, you have to know the right path to follow, and this knowledge comes from reading and deepening your understanding of the Bible.

Contact: To win in skiing, your skis should always be in contact with the snow. Anytime you're airborne, you lose time regaining your line and getting your skis pointed in precisely the right direction. Constant contact with God is also a necessity for a growing Christian. Bible study, prayer, and obeying God's instructions are all ways to keep from losing touch and missing out on the joy-filled life God intends his people to have.

I illustrated each of those points using films of my fourth-place finish at the Val d'Isere race.

But it wasn't until several weeks later, after the injury at Wengen and after I was home for therapy, that I got to know Gail, and that was almost as big of a challenge as winning a World Cup race.

One Sunday night, I was invited over to the Jespersens' house for a surprise engagement party for Gail's brother Brent. During the course of the evening, she was sitting on the couch, so I went and sat beside her.

"What do you do for a living?" I asked.

"I'm the only girl in a thirty-five-man office at O & S Construction. What do you do?" she returned calmly.

"Well, you know who I am. I came and spoke to your college and career group."

"Yes, but what else do you do?"

Good grief, I thought, *is she ever nervy. Here I am, the best skier in Canada, and she doesn't even*

*care about that. She wants to know what else I do,
as if skiing weren't worth discussing.* So we discussed farming. I couldn't believe her nonchalant attitude toward skiing, and I was impressed. I had to get to know this girl.

On Monday night, I called her up and asked for a date. She said no; she had voice lessons.

I called again Wednesday night. She had choir practice that night.

On Thursday night, I tried again. She had another choir practice.

"How many choirs are you in?"

She just laughed.

"Listen, if you don't want to go out with me, just say so. But if you do, when are you available?"

"I'm not available. I'm busy all the time."

But I wasn't ready to give up. If phone calls didn't work, I'd try something else. I was as determined to get together with Gail as I was to get my ankle back in shape, so I decided to combine the two goals. I found out where O & S Construction was from the telephone book, and the next Monday I put on my jogging suit and ran over there during office hours.

All hot and sweaty, I walked into the office and over to Gail's desk.

"What are you doing here?" she asked.

"Oh, I just happened to be in the area."

That line gradually came to be a standing joke, but it worked.

Apparently she got tired of saying no, and we eventually began seeing each other regularly. She never was overly impressed with Jim Hunter the skier, but I appreciated her interest in Jim Hunter the person.

From then on, no matter where I was around the world skiing, we wrote regularly and phoned frequently. My relationship with Gail also helped to remind me that there was more to life than skiing. But winning was still first on the list.

My ankle recovered in time for me to win the 1973 Canadian championship, edging out the up-and-coming racers like Doug Woodcock, Paul Carson, and David Irwin.

I found myself in an unusual position. Always before, I'd been one of the young guys. Now I was twenty years old and a veteran of the World Cup circuit. I was the one to beat for the younger Canadian skiers, and that made me feel a little strange. I still hadn't won a World Cup race, and I was the "old man" of the Canadian team. I began to wonder if the same thing would happen to me that had happened to the old guys I'd displaced.

The next season wasn't any encouragement. It was the one leading to the 1974 World Championships at Saint Moritz. I placed fourth in the giant slalom at Val d'Isere and fourth at the brand-new downhill run in Schladming, Austria—the fastest downhill in the world. I felt my skiing was coming together. A win couldn't be too far off. Then the hopes were dashed by the fall at Morzine.

For two years in a row, my well-laid plans to become a World Cup winner had been sabotaged by injuries. That wasn't in the script. My success story was supposed to include a World Cup win by this time. Now my leg was in a cast, and I wasn't sure if I'd be able to race again.

What could I have done differently? What does it take to win? I reviewed my formula so far—courage, desire, confidence, training, toughness, technique—what's left?

The question weighed on my mind as I watched the 1974 World Championships on television. Gustavo Thoeni made an amazing comeback in the second run to win the giant slalom. Behind by 2.5 seconds after the first run, Gustavo beat everyone by an incredible three seconds on the second run.

"That should be me," I said to myself over and over.

To me, my leg cast was a sign that my formula still had a few flaws, and if I ever skied again, I was determined to iron them out—whatever they were.

Fourteen
THE MISSING INGREDIENT

THE NEXT SUMMER, two things happened that I considered votes of confidence—one from God, one from the Canadian government. I interpreted them as signs that things were going to get better.

I was fully prepared to give up skiing when I flew home from Morzine with the ligament damage in my knee. My doctor told me that he wasn't sure whether to operate or not. He thought the best thing to do was put the leg in the cast for a couple months and see if it would heal on its own first. Then, if that didn't work, he would operate.

I told him, "If God wants me to ski again, he'll heal the leg. If he doesn't, then I won't." If the leg required surgery, I was ready to return to the farm full time.

Dr. Kastelin put on the cast, and I waited uncertain about my racing career. But within six weeks, the leg was healed. Dr. Kastelin said it was one of the quickest recoveries he'd ever seen. I think the explanation is simple—it was a miracle.

With a divine nod of approval like that, I

launched into my training program with eagerness. I was anxious to rehabilitate the knee, and I
was eager to see what God was going to do during
the next season.

I added a couple of new techniques to my training routine. First, I used the old boards and milk
cans that once served as the jump on the ice rink,
and I turned them into a starting ramp. I hauled
them into the barn loft, covered the ramp with
straw, and practiced my starts by the hour. Second,
on the back of the half-ton, I built a raised platform
that was just higher than the top of the cab. Wearing my downhill suit, I'd step into an old pair of
skis, crouch on top of the ramp, and dad would
drive about seventy miles an hour along the back
country roads around Shaunavon. It was the only
way I knew to simulate the wind resistance a racer
faces descending a mountain at those speeds. It
was an effective way to practice balancing in the
racer's crouch at high speed. With training like
that, my knee was feeling better and better.

The second vote of confidence came when Giles
Walker of the Canadian National Film Board
phoned me and asked if they could do a movie
about me during the upcoming season. The National Film Board produces films designed "to
interpret Canada to Canadians and to other countries." I knew the film would likely be shown on
Canadian national TV and be available through the
national film libraries after that.

"Why a film about me?" I asked.

"Because you're unique," Walker said. "You

stand up for what you believe, and you're not afraid to talk about what God means in your life. There aren't many athletes in Canada who do that."

"I'll do it under two conditions," I said. "I want you to show the struggles that amateur racers have—trying to compete with Europeans who have sophisticated videotape equipment, lots of coaches, wax testing, and summer racing facilities right in their own countries. Canadians don't have any of that. And second, I want my Christian testimony to be shown all the way through the film." Giles Walker agreed that they could do both of those things, and we arranged to do the film. I was really honored that the Canadian government was willing to do the project. Apparently at least the film board considered me a good enough skier to be the subject of a movie, and I was still Canada's number one skier. With that encouragement, I headed into Val d'Isere for the first race of the season.

Based on my FIS points, I was ranked number 18 in the world in the downhill, number 55 in the giant slalom, and number 103 in the slalom. And my near-win at Madonna convinced me that I could beat everybody if I could just put it all together.

I was healthy, I was confident, and I didn't see any reason why this couldn't be the year for the Canadians.

Val d'Isere was a rude awakening. I finished a disappointing twenty-eighth in the downhill—a full six seconds behind winner Franz Klammer of

Austria. None of the Canadians were even close to him.

The rest of the season followed that same frustrating pattern. At Saint Moritz, I was twelfth, and again Klammer won. At Garmisch, I was twenty-fifth; at Wengen, sixteenth; at Kitzbuhel, twenty-first—and on and on it went. Only at Innsbruck did I crack the top ten, but I was still well behind Klammer, who won an unprecedented six of seven downhills.

The giant slalom wasn't much better—my ninth at Madonna was the only time I cracked the top ten in that event, and in the slalom, I was never better than twenty-fifth.

A transformation had come over World Cup skiing, and it had taken the Canadians by surprise. The sport had passed the Age of Innocence. It was now a highly technical, highly specialized business.

The 1974-75 season was the first year of the skiing specialists. Always before, each skier had competed in all three events. This year, suddenly the only top skiers who competed in all three were Gustavo Thoeni, Walter Tresch, and myself. Everyone else specialized in only one or two events.

In the Val d'Isere giant slalom, for instance, Erwin Stricker, Franz Klammer, and I were the only downhillers to finish in the top twenty-five of the GS.

We Canadians were caught napping. We didn't know until we got into the season how widespread the specialization had become. Only eighteen World Cup skiers were competing in all three events, compared to sixty and up to eighty in each of the individual events.

Another transformation was the new importance of equipment. It had always been important before, but this year, certain things made a drastic difference—the new plastic suits, for instance.

The Italians had first introduced plastic downhill suits in 1970. They had never been a serious force in the downhill before, but suddenly the Italians had three racers who consistently finished in the top ten. Nobody dreamed it was because of the suits. But five years later, everyone was wearing them at Val d'Isere—everyone except the Canadians and Americans, that is. Apparently we were caught napping again. It began to look like we'd been asleep through quite a few things.

At the Val d'Isere downhill, everyone in the top twenty-five wore a plastic suit. They cut down on wind resistance and were very fast—also very dangerous. One skier who fell wearing a plastic suit slid 200 yards into the trees. The next race they were banned, officially, but they were still worn ... inside out. With the plastic side in, air still couldn't penetrate to slow the racer, but the fabric side out satisfied the FIS regulations.

We also learned that the Europeans had special arrangements with wax manufacturers for pretesting waxes. Manufacturer's representatives, experts in their field, would analyze the snow before each race and test air temperature, snow temperature, humidity, and granulation. The Swiss team even fed the data into a computer to determine the best wax combination for the specific snow conditions.

The Canadians, of course, had none of this. We didn't get the new plastic suits until the end of the year. And waxing was always left up to the coach. Scotty did a good job of judging the conditions, but he couldn't compete with experts and computers.

"You guys just have to ski faster" was all our coaches would say after a race. But that simply wasn't the case. No matter how fast we skied, we were at least three seconds behind. We'd always been a lot closer the year before.

Since I didn't feel that the coaches were getting us what we needed, I decided to take action myself. I couldn't do much about the waxes, but I did get myself one of the new downhill suits. I also bought a car to travel between races. All the Europeans were riding with manufacturers' representatives. Franz Klammer was flown to races in a helicopter, courtesy of Fischer skis. But the Canadians had a team bus. I couldn't understand why we had to ride for eighteen hours in a bus when the same trip by car would take ten. So I bought the car, so my time could be spent training and resting instead of being cramped up on the bus.

One day I heard that Klammer and the other Austrians had massages to relax their muscles after training. If it worked for them, it ought to work for me—so I started getting rubdowns each night after my exercises.

At one point in the season, I was so disgusted at

not coming close to winning that I decided the problem must be my skis. I'd run out of other ideas. Maybe Rossignols simply weren't as fast as Klammer's Fischer skis.

I got permission from Scott Henderson to try the new skis. After making one downhill training run on my Rossignols, I made a second using a pair of Fischers. The Fischers were only 0.07 seconds faster, though two runs is admittedly not a fair test.

That night Scotty told me he'd gotten a call from Luc Dubois, the Canadian alpine director. Apparently some of the suppliers for the Canadian team had heard I was thinking of changing brands, and they were so upset they threatened to stop their support of the team. Dubois told Henderson to straighten me out.

Since the difference between the two pairs of skis was so slight anyway, it wasn't worth the hassle to switch. I stayed with Rossignol.

I took a lot of heckling from the coaches and the other guys on the team about my search for the missing ingredient in my success formula. They considered all these factors gimmicks. They said the problem wasn't in the equipment; it was in my head.

If it was, I didn't know what it was nor what to do about it. I was in the best physical shape I had ever been in; I trained more than anyone else on the team; I certainly had the desire to win (some called it an obsession); and I knew I had enough ability—Madonna had proven that.

What did Klammer do that I didn't do? I kept

asking. The only thing I could figure was that he must use a different brand of toothpaste.

After the season was over, Giles Walker asked if I thought the season had been wasted.

"It's been a confusing season," I said. "It's one of those things, at least in my life, that with God's providence, I know he's got something in store for me. But I don't know what it is."

I was finding the mountain of competition higher and more treacherous than I'd ever realized from the valley floor below. What do you do when you don't know how you can improve any further? I had tried everything I could think of to be a winner. Maybe Scotty was right—maybe I'd been thinking too much. Whatever, I had pretty much run out of excuses.

Fifteen

KAMIKAZE CANADIANS

WHERE DO YOU TURN when you've been racing on the national team for six years, you're racing the best you know how, and it's still not good enough?

The 1975-76 season was an Olympic year, and I wanted to prove that I was a better skier now than in 1972. But I also told myself this was going to be my last year of racing.

Partly because of last year's dismal results, and partly because this was an Olympic year, the Canadian team officials put a lot of pressure on me to train full time during the summer. Dad was less than excited about not having me around to work, but eventually he agreed to give me the chance to go all out for the next season, so we hired a man to do my work on the farm.

At the summer training camps in South America and Europe, Scotty Henderson had us concentrate on downhill. Since everyone else in the World Cup was specializing, he decided we should, too. Why downhill? I'm still not quite sure, except that

Scotty was an old downhill racer and that's what he knew best, and over the past few years, our team had earned something of a "Kamikaze Canadian" reputation for our direct-assault approach to racing. Scotty felt that was where we had the best chance of breaking into the first seed.

Ken Read, David Irwin, and David Murray were concentrating almost exclusively on downhill. I was still going to compete in all three events, but we all felt the downhill was where our greatest hope of victory lay.

At the first World Cup race in Val d'Isere, Scott's strategy worked, but not the way I thought it was supposed to. In the downhill, Franz Klammer was finally beaten, and a Canadian won the race. It was the first World Cup victory for a Canadian male skier. The problem was, the winner wasn't me—it was Ken Read. I finished ninth.

It was a huge disappointment. Throughout summer training, because Read, Irwin, and Murray had been specializing totally in downhill, they had been beating me in the downhill training runs. But when Read beat me at Val d'Isere, it was a shock. I had always expected to be the first Canadian to win.

Two weeks later, when David Irwin won the downhill at Schladming, I began questioning my value to the team. I'd enjoyed my status as the Canadian team's ace, and now my ninths and fifteenths were looking rather feeble.

"Scotty," I said after the Schladming race, "it looks like you don't need me anymore now that

Read and Irwin are doing the winning."

"You shouldn't think that way, Jim," Scott said. "I knew you were going to. But you've got to realize that those two guys have been trying to gun you down for four years now. You should be proud of the fact that they knew if they could beat you, they could win a World Cup race."

Scotty went on to explain that I had been instrumental in breaking the European psychological barrier by consistently finishing near the top.

"Read and Irwin looked up to you as the one to beat," he said. "They knew that if they could start beating you in time trials, then they could win World Cup races."

Looking back, it seems funny that what Scott said had such an effect. He didn't say anything that I didn't already know, but just hearing him say it was an encouragement. I was able to return to racing with a new commitment toward winning.

"Yes," I admitted to myself, "they may wind up being better than I am in the downhill, but I'm going to give it my best shot anyhow. And I'll continue trying to pick off occasional World Cup points in the slalom and giant slalom events, too."

From that time on, my attitude was much better.

In the next two downhills, both of them at Wengen because there wasn't enough snow at Garmisch, I finished sixth and third. Then at Kitzbuhel, Austria, I finished seventh in the prestigious Hahnenkamm downhill and second overall behind Walter Tresch.

What made those races even more satisfying was

Jim muscles through a turn on his way to winning the first run of the 1972 Madonna di Campiglio World Cup giant slalom.

The Kamikaze Canadians (l. to r.) Ken Read, Jim Hunter, David Irwin, David Murray.

Above, Jim flies over a bump in the 1976 downhill at Wengen, where he finished third behind the Austrian ace, Franz Klammer, and Phillippe Roux (below).

that my brother Lorne had come over to see them. He was in Europe to try out for Holiday on Ice. For the first time, one of my family saw how big racing was in Europe. Almost fifty thousand people packed the slopes in Kitzbuhel to watch the Hahnenkamm. He saw why it's called "the Indianapolis of skiing." And he saw me win the second-place trophy.

Then came the Olympics, and as far as I was concerned, the timing was just right. My skiing was at its best. Because of the full summer of training, I felt I was in the best shape I'd ever been in. And my attitude was right. All systems were go for an Olympic medal.

The first thing the Canadians did when we got to Innsbruck was to go inspect the hills where we'd be racing. The downhill run had been sprayed with fifty thousand gallons of water, making it incredibly fast. It truly was "a run of fear," as they say on "Wide World of Sports." It was glare ice from top to bottom. I was ecstatic—the other racers weren't. I've always thrived on situations where other people were scared.

I remembered the first year the downhill was run at Schladming. At one point, a road cut across the course, and there was about a thirty-foot jump to clear it. No one knew what the jump was like—all three of the local skiers they'd sent down as guinea pigs to test it had wiped out, one guy nearly killing himself by falling short and landing on the road. After watching all this, they asked if any of us racers would be willing to give it a try. Andy Mill,

Erwin Stricker, and I immediately said yes. I don't know why the other two guys volunteered, but I had seen the fear in some of the other racers' eyes when they saw that jump. I wanted to be the first to make it. It would be a terrific psychological factor in the race, I was sure. So Mill, Stricker, and I all made the jump and survived.

"I'll race it," I said. I wasn't anybody to be reckoned with at that time, but I figured it couldn't hurt to go on record in favor of the jump.

The officials decided to go on with the race, and a couple of racers refused to enter the event. But I was eager to go. It was my kind of course—a terror—and I rose to the occasion and finished fourth, my best finish ever at that time.

Now at Innsbruck, I felt the same feelings. Runs of fear always brought out the best in me. The Innsbruck downhill was the perfect course for my first win, and the 1976 Winter Olympics was the perfect setting.

The training runs confirmed my thoughts. Out of six days of training runs, I was in the top five four times. On the fourth run, my time of 1:48.86 was the fastest of all training times. The favorites in the race were Bernhard Russi, who'd won the downhill in the 1972 Olympics, Franz Klammer, who'd been unbeatable last year and had returned to mere greatness this year, and Jim Hunter, the terror of the training runs.

The Olympic opening ceremonies at Innsbruck weren't anything like the experience in Sapporo. Here, I felt so much pressure I don't remember what went on. All I could think of was winning or losing that downhill. That was all that mattered.

After the last day of downhill training, I knew there was nothing else I could do until tomorrow. If I wasn't ready now, I never would be. But I couldn't relax. I spent the evening at the Olympic amusement area watching movies from the 1972 Olympics and playing the games in the arcade. Nothing, however, was able to take my mind off the downhill. I went to bed with sweaty hands and an unsettled stomach.

The next morning, Scott waxed the skis and told us to make a practice run on the warm-up slopes with our racing skis, a normal procedure so the wax would be ready for the race.

The training slope was crowded, but all the spectators were supposed to stay off to the sides to allow the racers to warm up. I took the lift to the top and then started down, building up speed gradually. My stomach was still tense. Four years worth of Olympic adrenalin had been building up for this downhill run. I was cruising about fifty miles an hour when I came to a right turn on the training hill.

As I leaned into the turn, suddenly a German spectator came skiing out in front of me. He glanced back, saw me, and frantically tried to get out of the way. But it was too late, and I was going too fast.

I passed over the tails of his skis, and my left shoulder hit him solidly in the back. I knocked him flying, and I went into a tailspin.

When the snow, skis, and bodies settled, I found I was unhurt, even though both of my skis and one of my poles were broken.

But I felt weak all over—totally drained. It was just like the feeling you have after narrowly avoiding an automobile accident. Memories of the cement floor of the farmhouse, the wipeout at Wengen, and the fall at Morzine all came flooding back. Thinking of what could have happened left me shaken.

The German spectator wasn't hurt, but my mental condition was undone. My adrenalin was spent forty-five minutes before the race began. I tried to relax and collect myself, but I couldn't work myself back to peak intensity. I felt it had already happened, and I was coming back down.

Fortunately, Scotty had already waxed my back-up skis, and I managed to borrow another pair of racing poles from Karl Anderson of the American team, but I was in no mental condition to race. I did the best I could, but I felt like I was out of control all the way down. I finished tenth.

Franz Klammer won, Russi was second, and Herbert Plank was third. Ken Read finished fifth, just ahead of Andy Mill, and David Irwin placed eighth, just behind Walter Tresch. Under the circumstances, I was more than happy with tenth place, though I was irritated that both Read and Irwin had beaten me, and I realized that any chance of an Olympic medal in an individual event was probably gone forever.

In fact, I had very little chance to get a medal in

the combined. Because we weren't practicing either the slalom or the giant slalom as a team, my results hadn't been very impressive so far. As the day drew nearer for the Olympic giant slalom, I grew more and more afraid of the course. It was very steep and very hard and should have been my kind of course, but my lack of practice made me feel awkward. I wasn't in control.

When the giant slalom was finally run, I was the only Canadian to finish—in distant twenty-second place. My combined times were ten seconds behind gold medal winner Heini Hemmi. I wasn't even close. But I learned something from the course that helped Kathy Kreiner of the Canadian women's team the next day.

I noticed that the guys who went down the course first got the better times. Often that isn't so. The first racer has to establish the line, and the others follow it. Generally the racers later in the first seed will get the best times.

But the Olympic giant slalom course was so steep and icy that the first skier had the advantage of the small skiff of snow that had accumulated overnight. It provided something extra for the ski edges to hang onto. After several racers went down, the skiff disappeared, the course started breaking up, and the times started getting worse.

The morning of the women's giant slalom, I was sitting in the cafeteria with the Russian hockey team, trying to converse. Most of the other athletes in the Olympic village would at least make an effort to communicate, but not the Russians. I wanted to talk to Alexander Yakushev, whom I considered one of the best hockey players in the world. He was a big guy—tall and muscular. I saw him devour four steaks in one sitting, but I couldn't get him to talk to me.

Just after breakfast was over, Kathy Kreiner walked over to me.

"Jim, I drew number one—what a bad number."

"Kathy," I said, looking her right in the eye, "you've got the best number on the hill. We raced the same hill yesterday, and I noticed the course started breaking up after the fourth or fifth guy."

I told her that the skiff of snow wouldn't slow her down; it would actually make the slope easier to handle.

"Do you really think so?"

"I know so. Look at the men's results. Gustavo Thoeni, Phil Mahre, and Ingemar Stenmark went first, and they wound up with the best first-run times. For the second run, they reversed the order, and Heini Hemmi was up front and he won."

"Yeah, I guess so," she said as she left.

I had nothing to do that day except practice slalom gates. So after a few runs, I went over to watch the women's giant slalom. George Duffield invited me to help broadcast the event for the CBC.

We made some introductory remarks as the forerunners came down. Theoretically, the forerunners are supposed to take off the soft snow, making it fair for everyone. But usually they don't ski as well as the competitors and don't get right beside the gates, so the snow removal job is incomplete. At the Olympics, since each country is allowed only four competitors in each event, they're able to use experienced World Cup racers as forerunners, but I still felt Kathy had the best chance from her number one spot.

When Kathy made her run, you'd never have known she didn't have a track to follow. She went zip, zip, zip through the gates and smoothly slipped through the finish.

Then the waiting began. Women have only one run in the giant slalom, but there were forty other racers to go.

After the fifth racer, Kathy's time was still the best, but the favorite, Rosi Mittermaier of Germany, still had to run. After another racer had come down, I told George, "Kathy's going to win—look at the way the course is deteriorating. Little lumps are starting to form, and people are having a hard time hanging on."

The one to wait for, however, was Rosi Mittermaier, who had won the downhill.

Then we saw Rosi come charging down the hill and zip through the finish. She was fast, but Kathy's time held up by one tenth of a second.

"So long, George," I said. "I'm going down to celebrate."

None of the men are allowed in the finish area, but I went looking for Kathy. I saw her and waved.

"Unbelievable!" she yelled.

She was jumping around and whooping it up. While the guard had his back turned watching her, I leaped the four-foot fence into the finish area.

"Kathy, I told you that you could do it!"

"I just can't believe it!"

We waited a couple minutes until Laurie Kreiner, Kathy's sister, made her run. When Laurie came in, she already had tears in her eyes, because from her position in the second seed she knew before she'd started that Kathy had won. It didn't seem to matter to Laurie where she finished—she was just excited Kathy had won.

When the race was finally over, everyone went crazy. The crowd was yelling and Kathy was ecstatic. I was the only Canadian man there—all the other guys had taken off after the downhill— and I was mildly irritated that they weren't there to share the moment with Kathy. Then I remembered a picture I'd seen of Billy McKay holding Nancy Greene on his shoulders after her 1968 Olympic wins. So I lifted Kathy up, people cheered, and the photographers went wild. I hadn't won a medal myself, but sharing that moment of victory with Kathy was almost as satisfying.

In the final event, the slalom, I finished twenty-second and again was just thankful to finish standing up. I had been scared of the course and woefully ill-prepared. I was sixth in the combined, way out of the picture for a medal, and my results were disappointing, but I didn't feel as bad about the whole situation as I expected to.

The week after the Olympics, I flew home for the Canadian championships, for the showdown with Read, Irwin, and the younger Canadian challen-

Kathy Kreiner and Jim celebrate her Olympic win.

gers. I won the slalom and giant slalom, finished second to Ken Read in the downhill, and won the Shell Cup as the overall Canadian champ.

There I finally felt that my work on all three events had paid off. After a year of doubt, I'd proven myself to be the best in Canada again, even if Read and Irwin did have World Cup wins.

I didn't have much time to savor the win, because the World Cup season still had a month to go, and I was starting to rethink my decision to quit after this year. Then two significant events happened that helped me make up my mind.

The first was a conversation I had with Spider Sabich while I was training in Aspen, Colorado, for the World Cup race there on March 12-14. Spider lived in Aspen and was training for his next race on the pro circuit. I had known Spider when he was still skiing on the American team.

He had always impressed me as an incredibly creative individual, someone who truly enjoyed living life to its fullest. In 1969, I had met him while in summer training in Portillo, Chile. He was on skis, wearing a long black robe and flapping his arms. He and Bernard Favre, the coach of the Spanish team in 1972, were making a videotape of "The Cybors Condor." Cybors, California, was Sabich's home town. For a confirmed stunt man like me, Sabich was a paradigm. He also impressed me with his relaxed attitude toward skiing—just the opposite of my intensity.

When we'd eat lunch at the top of the mountain, Spider would drink a whole bottle of wine. I was amazed. Not only was alcohol off my diet, but so was white bread, white sugar, and coffee. Spider didn't seem to restrict himself in any way. After lunch, he skied the rest of the afternoon and skied well. He never got too serious or too worked up, yet he skied so smoothly.

It amazed me. I attacked the mountain; he seemed to be a part of it.

After that year, I had raced against him a couple of times until he turned pro. At Aspen, we were both training at Buttermilk Mountain, and we rode the lift together.

"How's Claudine?" I asked. I knew he was living with Claudine Longet.

"Just fine," he said. "She's the greatest woman in the world."

"What are your plans for the future?"

"Listen, everything is planned. The next five years of my life are completely taken up."

"What do you mean?"

"Well, I've got my airplane, my house, my cars, a great woman, and I've got jobs and responsibilities that have me booked solid for the next five years."

"Sounds like you've got everything wrapped up pretty well."

"Yeah, I don't have too much to worry about anymore. I've got everything I need."

"Well, you know you don't live forever," I said. "You can't ever be sure of what will happen tomorrow."

"Aw, I don't have to worry. Everything's planned out."

We had plenty of time there on the lift, so I went ahead to say, "I don't mean to sound morbid, but what happens if you die? It could be tomorrow or it could be ten years from now, but a person needs to plan for that, too. You need to know where you're going when life's over."

"I don't have to worry about that stuff right now," Spider assured me. "Everything's taken care of for the next five years, and that's enough for me."

"Well, think about it sometime."

"Yeah, maybe sometime."

We made several more runs together before leaving, he for the pro races, me for the World Cup events.

A week later, I was in a car driving to Mont Sainte Anne, Quebec, for the World Cup finals, and I heard that Spider was dead, killed in an accident with a gun in his Aspen condominium. I was shocked. Only a week before, we had talked, and now he was gone. The thought stuck in my mind how short life is, how important Christ's message of love and forgiveness is, and how important it is that I share that message with my fellow skiers. I remembered the commitment I'd made at the kitchen table to be a missionary on the ski slopes. I hadn't been doing the job I could have. The experience with Spider left me thoughtful.

The second experience that caused me to rethink my decision to quit skiing was the race at Mont Sainte Anne.

In the giant slalom, I was twelfth after the first run. Then just before the second run, Chris Jones walked over to me. He was a ski coach and friend from Burke Mountain Academy. I hadn't even known he was there, but he came over to talk as I waited to start.

"Jim, why don't you make a run like I've seen you make at summer camp in Mammoth? Ski with total abandonment. Ski like you were shot out of a cannon and want to destroy the hill."

"Why not?" I said. "It's the last race of the season. What do I have to lose?"

So I blasted out of the start, and the next thing I knew I was at the finish—with the second-best time. The only guy to beat me on the second run was Heini Hemmi, the Olympic gold medal winner. I finished ninth in the event, but that second run turned me on for the special dual slalom competition the next day.

Dual slalom races pit man against man in parallel courses. You race twice, and the winner of the combined time difference advances.

In the first round of the dual slalom, I faced Gustavo Theoni, and I beat him. That brought on Rene Berthod, and I beat him. Then I had to take on Walter Tresch, and in the first run, I beat him by 0.350 seconds, but I knew that my course was the faster one. When we switched for the second run, the advantage would be his. As we flashed through the finish for the second run, Walter was just half a ski length in front of me. But the announcement came that Tresch had won by 0.500.

Walter and I looked at one another and shrugged. He said, "Well, I guess I won."

But I couldn't believe it, and neither could Walter. Half a ski length isn't half a second back.

Sure enough, a minute later the P.A. announced that there had been a timing error—Tresch had won the second heat by 0.050, and the winner was Hunter. That was more like it. I advanced to the semifinals to face the slalom ace from Sweden—Ingemar Stenmark.

I was psyched up. Beating Ingemar would be a coup. Unfortunately, Ingemar didn't relish the idea of an upset. He beat me by 0.187 in the first run and 0.318 in the second run. So I had to settle for beating Fausto Radici for the third-place trophy.

Placing third in the World Cup finals dual slalom was a great way to end what I considered a great season, Olympic disappointment notwithstanding. I'd finished tenth in the final World Cup downhill standings, and twelfth in the overall World Cup competition. I'd met the challenge of Read and Irwin and won the Canadian championship. At last, I thought, my act is coming together. I can't quit now. I've got to ski two more years and compete in the 1978 World Championships.

My dad wasn't keen on the idea. He had been disappointed when I'd done so poorly at the Olympics.

"Don't you think it's time you stopped chasing butterflies?" he asked. He said it was time to make a decision—was I going to be a skier or a farmer?

Lorne had successfully made the Holiday on Ice troupe as a featured performer with his own solo routine, but his first love was farming. Each summer, he was back on the farm. Why couldn't I be the same way?

I just couldn't bring myself to give up skiing. For eleven years, it had been what I'd lived for. It was what I worked ten months a year for. It was my mission, the place where we'd agreed that God wanted me. I couldn't retire yet. Now that I was starting to finish consistently in the top fifteen, I was sure winning couldn't be far away. Next year had to be the year I'd reach the top.

Unfortunately, sometimes a mountaintop looks a lot closer than it actually is.

Sixteen
ON MY OWN

EXCEPT FOR ONE THING, the 1976-77 season was a disaster. The year that was supposed to be simply wasn't. Maybe dad was right—butterflies are mighty elusive. Yet, the distasteful season brought about a major change in my life, one that I feel God had planned.

The only bright spot of the year was getting married to Gail in August. For the past three years, I felt I'd been singlehandedly underwriting Bell Telephone with my transatlantic calls. Gail had been a real source of strength for me throughout the disappointment of the Olympics, the injuries, and the pressure to win. I came to rely on her support. Oddly enough, however, our marriage turned out to be one of the factors in the disastrous 1976-77 season.

The problem actually started three weeks before our wedding. My brother Lorne was getting married on July 30, and the day before, he and I were having one of our frequent wrestling matches out in the yard, which was rutted from recent rains.

Suddenly, my foot caught in a rut just as Lorne's weight shifted. I fell, and my right knee, the same one I'd hurt at Morzine, sent stabbing pains throughout my leg. I tried to stand up, but I couldn't.

"Lorne, I've ruined my knee," I said through clenched teeth.

We tried to straighten the leg, but I couldn't even do that—it was locked in a bent position. By the time we got to Dr. Kastelin, the knee was puffed and swollen. He relaxed it and got the knee to straighten out. But the news wasn't good.

"I'm afraid we're going to have to operate," Dr. Kastelin said. "Your miracle knee came back once, but this time I'm going to have to open it up for surgery."

Since I had to be in Lorne's wedding the next day, Dr. Kastelin put a temporary cast on the leg so I could stand up at the ceremony. But the following Monday, I had surgery for torn cartilage. After staying a week in the hospital to recover, I returned to the farm and did some swathing in the wheat fields for a couple weeks before our wedding.

I got out of the cast just in time to be married. I sang to Gail as she came down the aisle, and then we sang to each other. Nancy Greene, who was now married to Al Raine, was there with her husband to watch us say our vows. People said it was a fairytale wedding.

Because of the demands of harvest, we couldn't take an extended honeymoon. We spent three days

During the off-season, Jim and his wife Gail often sing and speak in churches and youth meetings.

in Kalispell, Montana, before returning to the farm.
By now the farm had grown to 3,000 acres. It was a
big business. Dad was suggesting more and more
strongly that I farm full time. There was no way I
could train like I did last year.

Then in September Scott Henderson stopped by
the farm to visit, and the tension with the team
began. Since I had been in the cast and unable to
work out, I had quickly gained weight, and I was
up to 200 pounds, about 25 pounds more than
normal.

"Why haven't you been at any of the training
camps this summer?" he asked.

"I've got to farm and earn a living somehow," I
said.

"Are you going to race this year?"

"I don't know."

"We're having a training camp in Europe starting October 5, and if you're going to be on the team,
you'll have to be there."

"Scotty, I'm not in shape—I can't even ride my
bike ten miles to Shaunavon. I've been working on
my knee like I did in 1974, but I'm still overweight
and out of condition."

But Scott urged me to report to the camp anyway.
He didn't want me to start the season behind the
others.

When I got to Europe and began skiing, however,
I felt like I was three years behind everyone else. I
couldn't keep up. The coaches were paying more
attention to the others than to me. At least I felt that
way because the team had changed so much—

more racers and less personal attention. Even though I'd had my best season ever last year, I felt like I was a rookie. I was dying—out of condition, with stale technique and poor timing. Everyone thought I'd be ready, but I wasn't, and I didn't get any encouragement from the coaches. I felt worthless.

Trying to compete when I didn't have the physical resources to do so was totally demoralizing. Depression set in. Even my relationship with God went sour—it didn't seem to mean anything anymore.

When the camp ended, I came home and then flew with Gail to California. Gail's brother Keith lived in Los Angeles, and while staying with them, I started a crash training program. I had a month to get ready for Val d'Isere. I still felt angry with the Canadian national team. I felt used and abandoned. When you got hurt, no one was there to help you pick up the pieces. No one was there to advise me on rebuilding my knee. It seemed that once you're hurt, you have to work yourself back into shape with no help or encouragement from the team, and then once you're fit, they're willing to associate with you again. I tried to channel my anger into my training routine.

I succeeded in getting my weight down to 190 by the time the season started, but that was still 15 pounds overweight, and I still didn't have the stamina I knew I'd need. Gail and I flew to Europe, and I didn't feel ready.

When we got there, the conflicts began immediately. Scotty seemed like a totally different person than I had known the previous years. He took charge, exerting his authority in places where the skiers had been independent before.

The first conflict was about Gail coming with me.

"I don't think you should bring Gail along on the circuit," Scott said.

"Why not?"

This was a complete surprise for me. The irony of the situation was that for years I had been told that marriage would be good for me, that it would help burn up the excess energy I spent doing extra workouts. Since I didn't party and chase women like some of the other skiers on the circuit, they told me that I ought to get married so I could work off my sexual energy that way. Now the team did a complete turnaround.

"I don't think you should have Gail around because it will affect your concentration, and it will bother the other guys on the team," Scott said.

"What do you mean, 'bother the other guys on the team'?" I asked. "They all know Gail and get along OK."

"But I think they'd feel inhibited with her around. The guys couldn't be themselves."

What he meant, of course, was that they wouldn't feel free to use foul language, tell crude stories, and describe their latest good time. I was disgusted. I didn't say anything, but if not being able to tell dirty stories affects a person's skiing, I considered it a sign of real mental weakness.

It was unfair, but nevertheless I arranged for Gail to have separate accommodations and to stay away from the team, especially on race days, as Scotty requested.

Even with Gail staying out of sight, the season was a disaster for everyone. I was still trying to lose weight, eating only 900 calories a day (3,500 are normal). But I continued to feel heavy and slow in the races. I couldn't move. I don't know what the problem was with the other guys, but they weren't getting any results either.

We were all six seconds behind the winner at Val d'Isere—a humiliation. At Val Gardena, we were all eight seconds out. We became the joke of the circuit. Not a single Canadian placed in the top fifteen. People began to ask, "What's happened to the Canadians?" We didn't know. We started suspecting a European conspiracy to give us inferior equipment.

The night after the Val Gardena fiasco, Ken Read and I were sitting in the hotel lounge watching the reruns of the race on TV. After most everyone else had gone to eat dinner, I saw a man across the room who looked strangely familiar, but I couldn't quite place him.

Then it dawned on me—he worked for Toko Wax. I'd heard that Toko had introduced some new waxes this year, but the Canadians were still using the same ones as the year before. So I spoke in German and asked the man, "Does Toko have any new waxes?"

"*Ja.*"

"How many kinds?" I asked.

"Seven."

As I turned to translate the conversation to Kenny, the man rose to leave. Kenny said, "Ask him why he didn't give us the new waxes."

So I yelled after him, "Why didn't you give them to us?"

"You never asked," he said over his shoulder. He gave us a little grin as he walked away.

After that, Kenny and I were convinced that the European manufacturers didn't care if the Canadians had the best equipment. The manufacturers had arrangements with the European teams to test the latest products, but the Canadians would have to take the initiative if they wanted the same goods.

When we did ask the Canadian team officials to get the new products for us, they refused to let the company representatives help us. They felt Scott was doing a good enough job, and they didn't want a European manufacturer's representative making the waxing decisions.

Granted, Scotty did a good job with the waxes he had. But when he had only four waxes to work with, and the competition had seven others and knew how to mix them in different combinations for the various snow conditions, it put us at a definite disadvantage.

The situation created a lot of dissension. The racers began to lose faith in the coaches and the officials. When you get yourself mentally and physically prepared for a race, when you give maximum effort, and still wind up eight seconds out, it's a disgrace. We realized we wouldn't be competitive without help from the Europeans. But because of national pride, ignorance, or whatever the reason, the Canadian officials were determined to win without European help. The racers knew it couldn't be done.

The season went from bad to worse. Last year, I hadn't been more than three seconds behind the winners. This year, I was never closer than six seconds and never placed higher than twenty-eighth.

It all came to a head in Kitzbuhel. My parents had come over to Europe for the first time. Since Lorne was skating with Holiday on Ice, and I was skiing, they thought it was a good time for their first overseas vacation. Mom, dad, Lorne, and Gail were all there to see the race.

Finally my parents could see the massive crowds of European racing fans, they could see the old traditions surrounding the running of the Hahnenkamm, and they could see where I'd finished second to Walter Tresch for the overall trophy last year. Unfortunately, this was 1977, the year nothing was going right.

I finished forty-second, a full eleven seconds behind the winner, and a Russian skier beat me. My timing was off; my coordination was off. The whole thing was a disgrace.

After the slalom race on Sunday, Scotty came up, and I noticed he looked pale. I wondered if he were sick.

"Jim, we've got to have a little talk."

We agreed to meet that night in the hotel. I knew something was going to have to be done. Scott was frustrated with me, and so was I. I didn't like my finishing forty-second any better than he did.

That afternoon Lorne, dad, and I got together to discuss what could be done. We sort of half-decided that the best thing I could do was to return home to get back in shape. There really wasn't any opportunity to regain my technique and conditioning while I was on the circuit. But we decided to wait and see what Scott said.

The meeting with Scott and the other coaches was "open and frank," which is diplomatic language meaning that we had strong disagreements. Scott wanted to know why Gail had come to the race.

"Scotty, for the past month, she's been visiting friends in Germany. She's been away from the team. I told you last Friday that my parents were going to be here for this race. Why shouldn't Gail be here with them to see the race, too?"

Scotty repeated his opinion that Gail prevented the guys from being themselves.

"Listen, Scotty," I said. "You've got your wife along. If Sully can be here, why can't Gail?"

"Sully has team responsibilities—she handles the videotaping and other details."

I realized he had a point, and it was useless to argue.

Then the coaches said the Canadian team wanted me to meet three demands. First, that I make a full commitment to racing. Second, that I not have any outside interferences so I could race all year long. And third, that I leave Gail at home.

"What kind of marriage would that be?" I asked.

"Jim, you just can't race your best if you're worrying about your wife."

I knew it was time for a decision.

"Scotty, I know I've been disgracing the team with my performances on the slopes—we're not having the kind of year we had last year, and it looks like we're losing our grasp on things. Maybe the best thing for me to do is go back home, work like mad for the next month to get in shape, and rejoin the team after the Canadian championships."

Both Scotty and Andrzej Kozbial, the team program director, agreed that this might be the best solution.

It was a long, hard trip back across the Atlantic. Each of the members of the team had told me they were sorry to see me leave. Sully Henderson and Steve Podborski both had tears in their eyes as we said good-bye in Kitzbuhel. Read, Irwin, and Murray all wished me the best. I was close to tears, but I had a sense of peace about the decision—I knew it was the right one.

When I landed in Toronto on my way home, the Toronto paper had a front-page story—"Jim Hunter, Rebel, Kicked Off National Team." It was the first time my name had ever been on page 1, but there it was, complete with a quote from Scott Henderson saying I was causing dissension on the team.

I couldn't believe it. Immediately I called Ed Champaigne, the business manager of the national team.

"What's going on?" I demanded. "I wasn't kicked off. I realized I wasn't competitive, so I came home to train."

Ed couldn't give me an answer, so I called several other national team officials. Some hemmed, some hawed, but no one could give me a satisfactory answer. I was miffed with the whole organization. I found out later a European writer had overdone his story.

Dad argued even more strongly that I was chasing butterflies with the national team. They didn't give me the respect dad thought I deserved, and he thought I might as well give up skiing. I was starting to listen, but couldn't quite accept such a drastic solution yet.

A couple of weeks later, I was invited to Toronto to see the pro races. I looked up Alan Eagleson, an attorney I had met at the Innsbruck Olympics. I knew he was Bobby Orr's agent and had a reputation of being able to make tough decisions quickly and wisely. He had told me at Innsbruck that if I ever turned pro or needed help with contracts to let him know and he'd be glad to help. So I explained the mess with the national team and told him I wanted to turn pro.

"It would be a mistake to turn pro right now," Eagleson said. "First of all, in the eyes of Canadian racing fans, justifiably or not, you are the bad guy—the black sheep who left the national team.

Secondly, if you turn pro and do poorly, everyone will think the national team was right—you were no good and should have been kicked off. And if you turn pro and succeed, then you'll still have to live with your failure on the national team, and you'll just make the pro circuit look shabby.

"No, the thing to do is get back in shape, win the Canadian championship, prove you're still the best in Canada, and then turn pro."

I had to agree he was right. Then I asked Eagleson to help me straighten out the newspaper reports. He and I sat down with Andrzej Kozbial to verify that I had not been kicked off the team. Andrzej agreed, and he issued a news release stating that the earlier reports out of Europe were in error. But as usual, retractions don't undo all the damage caused by the initial story. People continued to ask me why I'd been kicked off the team. The only thing I could do to clear my name was to win the Canadian championship.

The 1977 Shell Cup Canadian National Championships were held in Mont Sainte Anne, Quebec, the same place I had done so well last year. After a month of intense training, running, lifting weights, riding my bike, and skiing on the slopes around Calgary, I was back in shape. The month off had also done wonders for my attitude.

Only two events made up the Shell Cup competition that year—the slalom and the giant slalom. Since the national team had been largely concentrating on downhill, my month at home working on the slalom and giant slalom should have put me at a decided advantage. I felt prepared for the giant slalom, but I still hadn't gotten my touch back in the slalom. That worried me a bit.

The giant slalom was run first, and I was ready to compete. For years Scott Henderson had been telling me that suppleness is the key to racing, not brute strength. Fluid, relaxed moves are what a ski racer is after. If you hit hard in any one spot, you lose momentum. Power has to be used in a subtle way, with a very fine touch. My problem generally was being too powerful. But for the Shell Cup, I felt smooth. I had the fine touch. And I won the race by 2½ seconds over David Murray and Steve Podborski.

I was halfway to the championship. But I was still feeling shaky about the slalom. As it turned out, I had good reason to feel shaky. Steve Podborski, a newcomer to the Canadian national team, was skiing very well and won the slalom event. But I managed a second-place finish about 0.8 seconds back, and that was close enough. I had hung on to win the overall trophy.

The Shell Cup was mine. It was an intensely satisfying win. After having to leave the team, after being criticized on page 1 of the paper, after not being allowed to have my wife accompany me during the season, I felt a profound sense of accomplishment. I had vindicated myself, proving I was still Canada's best.

Unfortunately, the win didn't make things any better with the Canadian national team. Two World Cup races remained in this year's

The 1977 Canadian national team included (from left) program director Andrzej Kozbial, racers Rob Safrata, Jim Hunter, Ken Read, David Murray, downhill coach Wayne Gruden, and head coach Scott Henderson.

Jim raises the Shell Cup after coming back to win the 1977 Canadian championship.

competition—one at Sun Valley, Idaho, the other at Heavenly Valley, California—and I rejoined the team for those.

At Sun Valley, the two events were the slalom and giant slalom. I finished both as the top Canadian, but I was still far from World Cup form. I still felt out of control. I was twenty-first in the slalom, way behind Phil Mahre of the United States, who won easily. And in the giant slalom, Ingemar Stenmark took the top spot, and I was a distant twenty-ninth.

The final straw came in Heavenly Valley, where a downhill was to be run. I walked into the ski room to get my equipment, and it wasn't there. But Luc Lajuenese, my ski rep, was.

"Where's my downhill equipment, Luc?"

"I don't know."

"Why not?"

"I was told you're not racing downhill anymore."

"Listen, I was a downhill specialist. I was the best in Canada for the last four years. What do they mean I'm not racing downhill anymore?" I knew I didn't have much of a leg to stand on because of my miserable results this year, but then, everyone's results had been miserable.

"The national team's decision was that you wouldn't race downhill," said Luc.

Period. End of conversation. And, as far as I was concerned, the end of my relationship with the national team. It was a severe disappointment—I couldn't understand why I didn't get the chance to come back after I'd proven myself at the Canadian championships.

There was nothing to do but go home. For about three weeks, I did little but read my Bible and pray. I felt abandoned and rejected. I told myself I'd raced for my country in two Olympics and had skied with intensity for the national team each year in between. Now that didn't seem to be good enough—if I wasn't willing to give up the farm and leave my wife at home, I couldn't ski.

"Why is this happening, Lord?" I prayed. "You were supposed to make things right with the team, not make them worse."

I guess the team figured that I was twenty-four years old, that I'd had my chance, and that it was time to make room for younger guys. I remembered the changes on the 1971 team that had given me my opportunity, but it didn't make me feel any better.

Gradually, as I studied my Bible, I came to an odd realization. Maybe . . . just maybe . . . God didn't require his people to be winners.

As I'd been climbing my mountain, straining for the summit and a World Cup crown, I'd been sure God expected me to win. I felt I was handcuffing God if I didn't make it. But perhaps he had other ways of using me . . .

One passage in the Bible impressed me with what God really considered important. In Luke 5, Simon Peter and his partners James and John had been fishing all night, without success. As they were washing their nets, Jesus walked to where their boats were beached.

"Put out into deep water, and let down the nets for a catch," Jesus said.

Simon answered, "Master, we've worked hard all night and haven't caught anything."

But eventually the fisherman followed Jesus' suggestion and tried again. This time they caught so many fish that their nets began to break and their boats almost sank from the weight.

Simon Peter knelt in front of Jesus and said, "Go away from me, Lord; I am a sinful man."

Then Jesus said, "Don't be afraid; from now on you will catch men." And the three men left their nets to follow Christ.

I knew exactly how Peter felt—I'd been fishing for a World Cup win not just all night, but for seven years. And I was surprised at Jesus' reaction. What did Jesus say to beaten fishermen? He didn't tell them they were failures. He didn't tell them to give up. He told them to try again. But even more important than that, he showed them that being fishers of men was what he was really interested in, more than fishing (or skiing) success. I began to feel a sense of calm.

And when I read Philippians 4:7—"And the peace of God, which passes all understanding, will keep your hearts and minds in Christ Jesus"—I knew what it meant, because I was experiencing it.

I knew I had to reorder my priorities. For too long, winning had been my god. Just because I was a child of God was not a divine dictate to win. There were more important things in life than winning. Once you win, what then? People only expect you to win again. After years of climbing that mountain, I realized I was on the right slope, but maybe approaching it from the wrong direction.

Yes, I was still a skier and wanted to win, but a new goal began to form in my mind: to introduce other people to Christ, to help them experience the inner calm he offers. That was the mountain worth climbing. I also had a new desire to pass on what I'd learned about skiing to younger skiers. For years, as I had climbed my mountain, my eyes had been focused only on the summit. Now I understood that God wanted me to look around at the others on the slope and give them a hand upward.

A couple of weeks before, I had been ready to give up skiing. Now I was convinced that God had a purpose for me, but as Jesus had told Peter, I needed to shove out into the deep water and cast my nets.

I couldn't think of any deeper water than professional ski racing.

Seventeen
A ROOKIE AGAIN

PROFESSIONAL SKI RACING is a relative newcomer to the world of sports. The 1977-78 season was only the ninth of its existence. Like golf and tennis before it, pro skiing started modestly and gradually built up. As a rookie, I benefited from people like Billy Kidd, Spider Sabich, Jean-Claude Killy, and most recently Henri Duvillard, who had won past World Pro Skiing championships and added respectability to the circuit. This season would be the biggest ever—thirteen weekends of racing, and each week's winner could take home over $10,000.

A new event was going to be introduced to the pro circuit this year—a downhill. In years past, the pro tour had become well known for its man-against-man competition in the slalom and giant slalom, but this year, the always innovative founder and president of WPS, Bob Beattie, decided to add "a short, punchy downhill."

As I flew to Aspen, Colorado, for the first pro race of the year, I wondered how the pro circuit, and particularly the customized downhill, would differ from World Cup racing. I knew the pro circuit was geared for the North American audience, and that meant the focus was on entertainment. Fans on this side of the Atlantic aren't as well versed in the intricacies of skiing as their European counterparts. Technically tricky runs aren't appreciated as much as simply putting on a good show. Therefore, pro runs are about one third of the length of World Cup races but demand more speed and more strategy.

The dual-course, one-on-one format in the slalom and giant slalom is a real crowd pleaser, and the artificial jumps they've added in the middle of the runs make the race even more colorful. But the format means that the winning pro must race ten runs before the last competitor is eliminated. It's a lot more demanding than the single giant slalom run per day that I was used to in the World Cup.

Side-by-side racing was too dangerous for the new downhill event, however, so Beattie opted for a shorter downhill run to let the crowd see more of the good stuff from the bottom of the hill.

Beattie hadn't told the racers about the new downhill idea until the end of November, only three weeks before the first event was scheduled at Aspen on December 15. I got Beattie's letter while I was on the farm in Saskatchewan.

Early that spring, my sister Marilyn had discovered she had a brain tumor. Mom and dad spent the summer with her in Edmonton while Gail and I ran the farm by ourselves. We were greatly relieved when surgery seemed to take care of the tumor.

But working full time on the farm meant I couldn't train as extensively as I wanted for the pro season. I was still overweight from the year before, so I started fasting two, sometimes three days a week. After a full day in the fields with no food, I could feel the pounds being shed. By fall, I was back to my normal 176, yet I knew I hadn't had the complete, full-time training I'd had before the 1976 season.

In October, after harvest was in, Gail and I flew to Tignes, France, so I could train with the Rossignol team. I'd signed a contract with the Rossignol Ski Company when I announced my decision to turn pro. I now joined Tyler Palmer, Otto Tschudi, and the other pros who skied on Rossignol skis. We were being coached by Jean-Pierre Monnot.

The first five days were spent simply free-skiing. I was surprised that we didn't start out with gates right away—that's what we had done on the Canadian national team. Instead we slowly got the feel of the snow, and I was grateful for the gradual reintroduction to my skis.

While we were dryland training one day, some French reporters asked Monnot about the team and specifically about me. Monnot said, "If Jim Hunter had been coached by the French or the Austrians during his amateur career, he would have been a world champion."

I asked Monnot why. What would European coaches have done differently?

He said, "No one trained you right. Your coaches only worked with you while you were practicing downhill runs, giant slalom courses, or slalom gates. Ski racing is much more than that."

I discovered what Monnot meant. He monitored my whole day. He spent time with me setting up a training program to follow during my morning and evening exercise routines. He was concerned about my diet. He kept me from being overactive. I could feel myself gaining new confidence and competence as Monnot oversaw my training. By limiting my extra work, I found I had more energy while I was on the snow. Finally I realized what Killy had meant years ago when he said, "Energy is the key to racing."

When the Rossignol team finished the dryland training and started practicing slalom gates, I felt faster than ever before. When the pros from the Salomon team arrived—among them Doug Woodcock, Jean-Pierre Hefti, and Josef Odermatt—we set up a dual course and had some competition.

I raced everyone I could, and managed to beat all comers. But I hadn't raced Odermatt. He had finished as the runner-up to Duvillard on the pro circuit last year, and with Duvillard's retirement, Odermatt was the favorite to win it all this year. I wanted to see what I could do against him, but at the same time, I was terribly nervous about it. Watching him, I could see that he was very sure of himself—every move, on or off his skis, was made with confidence.

"He knows exactly where he's going," I said to myself. "I doubt if I can beat him, but one of these days we'll find out."

A couple of days later, we found out. I was through practicing for the day, and I had my skis over my shoulder and was heading home. I passed Odermatt as he was heading to the start of the slalom course.

"Want to run?" he asked.

"No, I'm finished for the day."

"What's the matter? You can only get beat."

His cockiness irritated me. I knew he was trying to goad me, and I also knew he had succeeded.

"All right, you're on," I said.

I was so determined to wipe that self-assured grin off Odermatt's face that I forgot that the skis I was putting on were my practice pair, not my racing skis. Even if I had noticed, however, I probably would have gone against Odermatt. I was determined to blow him away.

Starting techniques in the pros differ from those used in World Cup racing. The pro racer has to have lightning-quick reflexes to get out of the start as soon as the metal gates swing open. In amateur racing, you have to have a good start, too, but it doesn't matter whether or not you start instantaneously when you hear the "go" signal. The clock doesn't start running until you trip the wand. In pro racing, you start as soon as the gates open. You have to anticipate the split second they open, yet not hit them prematurely, or they jam shut. Some amateur racers have a hard time adjusting to this difference.

All week I'd been working on my anticipation and starting technique. When the doors swung open, Odermatt and I leaped out as if released from the same spring. We were right together as we hit the first bump, but as I landed, both skis came off. I pitched forward, and I put out my hands to break the fall. I slid face-first several yards down the mountain.

When I got up, I didn't feel any pain, but I had a strange feeling that something was wrong, even though I didn't know what it was. As I reached down to pick up my pole, I found out—I couldn't move my right thumb. I pulled off the glove, and the thumb was already starting to swell.

It was a long walk the rest of the way down the course. I knew the thumb was at least seriously sprained, and probably broken.

When I got to the hospital, the doctor took X rays, glanced at them quickly, and said, "We operate tomorrow at nine o'clock. That's all. Good night." And he walked out without giving me a chance to say a word.

So I phoned Otto Tschudi, who spoke French. He did some checking around, and found out that the doctor was a little eccentric. If any surgery was going to be done, I didn't want a strange doctor doing it. At six the next morning, we walked out of the hospital and made our getaway. By nine, I was on a plane bound for Canada. Even though training camp wasn't over for five more days, I had to leave. The thumb demanded immediate attention.

Gail and I didn't arrive in Toronto until after the last plane to Calgary had already left. We had to spend the night in the airport, and by now the painkillers had worn off and the thumb was killing me. Every time I moved it, the pain made me shudder.

The next day, we arrived in Calgary about noon, went immediately to the hospital, and the thumb underwent a two-hour operation that afternoon. It was broken in four places, and three two-inch pins had to be inserted to hold the bone back together. Dr. Kastelin put the whole thing in a cast and told me it would take two months to heal.

"But I've got to race December 15."

"I'm afraid it won't be ready by then," he said.

But a couple weeks later, Dr. Kastelin decided he could take the pins out and put the hand into a plastic working cast. After that, I started working out again—with weights, riding my bike, and free-skiing around Calgary. I also started running with a man who didn't know a thing about ski racing, but who taught me something that I would put to use at Aspen.

Bob Cleveland was the forty-three-year-old associate pastor of First Alliance Church in Calgary. He had just come recently, and since Gail and I had been on the farm all summer, I really didn't know him. But I'd heard he ran ten miles, three days a week.

"Nobody that old can run that far," I said when I heard it.

Bob proved me wrong. He was tall and lean, with slicked-back hair—hardly the image of an athlete. He'd grown up on a farm, and recently, when he went back to visit and help bale hay, he was dismayed at how out of condition he was and decided to do something about it. He started running, and maintained the discipline until he could log ten miles nonstop every other day. We began running together.

It was on our jaunts that I learned another discipline that Bob maintained—Scripture memorization. He would work on memorizing verses from the Bible while he ran—he said it made the miles go by faster. I wanted to try it.

Since I'd been discouraged by Dr. Kastelin's initial prediction about my thumb, I'd mentioned to Bob that I was thinking of not skiing this year. In one of my lower moments, I told him maybe I shouldn't ski at all. Bob suggested we memorize Colossians 3:22-24, and we did. It was Bob's way of reminding me I had a contract with Rossignol, an obligation that God expected me to fulfill to the best of my ability. So as we ran we recited, "Servants, obey in all things your masters according to the flesh; not with eyeservice, as menpleasers; but in singleness of heart, fearing God: And whatsoever ye do, do it heartily, as unto the Lord, and not unto men; Knowing that of the Lord ye shall receive the reward of the inheritance: for ye serve the Lord Christ."

I continued to ski at Paskapoo, near Calgary, and Gail and Bob Cleveland would film me. Studying the films, I decided I didn't look that bad, considering that I hadn't trained all summer, that I'd been on skis only six days in Europe before I broke my thumb, and that I was still in a working cast. I didn't have any illusions about my chances at Aspen, though. When December 12 came, I decided to go on and compete, make a fool of myself, get it over with, and slowly regain my form as the season went on.

The only hope I had was the fact that I finally realized my lack of training wasn't as big a curse as I'd always considered it. At least I was well rested.

Prior to the Aspen downhill, we had three days to train on the course. But during the six time trials, I wasn't even close. It was obvious that I was rusty. The night before the race, I was so discouraged and afraid I was going to humiliate myself that I couldn't sleep. So I called Bob Cleveland.

"Bob, I'm a downhill racer right off the World Cup circuit, and I'm going to lose."

"Jim," he said, "I want you to go to bed and forget about this nonsense of doing poorly. What you need is a good night's sleep. Turn off the TV. Don't even do your regular Bible study. Just look up one verse, and then go to bed."

The verse was Isaiah 26: 3—"Thou wilt keep him in perfect peace, whose mind is stayed on thee: because he trusteth in thee."

As I looked over those words, a surge of confidence welled up inside me. I just let my eyes rest on that verse, soaking up its meaning. I had it memorized before I fell asleep.

The next day, I awoke nervous but ready to run the downhill. The WPS had devised a format to make the new event as spectator-oriented as possible. Thirty-two racers were qualified. After the first run, the field would be cut to sixteen. The sixteen survivors would make a second run. But unlike most downhills, the racer with the slowest time in the first run would start first, and the fastest man would start last. It makes for a handicap system of sorts, because ski racing courses become more rutted and slower with each run. Fastest combined time for the two runs would win, and that meant the issue wouldn't be decided until the last man was down.

The downhill course on Buttermilk Mountain was deliberately made easy—a picnic by World Cup standards. The run was only 6,000 feet long, with a vertical drop of 1,200 feet, and the only thing that brought the racing speeds up to 60 miles per hour was the relatively straight course. The most dangerous part of the course was the stopping area, because there wasn't much of it.

Since this was the first downhill for the pro circuit, some of the racers didn't have downhill equipment. There was something of a scramble for skis, helmets, suits, and poles, especially by the racers whose sponsors didn't make downhill gear. Fortunately, Rossignol did.

I had two downhill suits, one an old suit from my days on the Canadian national team that had the fish gills backwards. Fish gills are the textured part of the fabric, slick on one side, to allow for least wind resistance. When we'd first gotten the defective suits, we were sure it was another European plot to slow us down. The material didn't channel the wind the direction it was supposed to go. My other suit looked almost the same, but the fish gills were the right direction. At Aspen, when Doug Woodcock told me he didn't have a downhill suit, I gave him one of mine. On the race day, I was dismayed to discover that I had given him my good suit—I had to wear the one with the fish gill problem. I tried to find Woodcock, but he was nowhere to be found.

As I rode the lift to the top of the hill, I thought, *Not only is my head going against me, but now my suit is, too.* A case of nerves set in, and again I was sure I was going to make a fool of myself.

When I got near the starting area, I stayed away from the other racers. Off by myself, I crouched down on my skis and put my head in my hands. *Thou wilt keep him in perfect peace. . . .* The words of last night came back to me. I repeated them over and over. Slowly the nerves subsided. For the first time I realized that God was with me, and that fact wouldn't change even if I bombed out on this run. God's love didn't depend on my finishing first. A bit of that perfect peace settled in my stomach and eased some of the tension.

When my turn came, I took off, skating and pushing with my poles. The run wasn't too steep, and I headed down the fastest line I could find. A few rocks were visible above the snow. I worried about catching an edge on one of them and flipping over. I tried to put the thought out of my mind. *Thou wilt keep him in perfect peace. . . .*

Then it was over. I flashed through the finish so fast I couldn't stop in time. I went over a four-foot drop out into the bushes.

As I turned around, the first thing I saw was Tommy Waltner, the Rossignol rep who worked on my skis, jumping over the embankment, running toward me, waving his beer can and yelling, "You did it! You did it!"

I had run the course in 1:19.779—the fastest time of the day. It was, however, only 0.012 seconds ahead of rookie Steve Devin, and 0.059 seconds ahead of Rudd Pyles, the six-year pro veteran and local favorite from Copper Mountain, Colorado.

Even though I had won the first run, I hadn't felt a total release. I had been holding back, a little scared of the rocks. The day was beautiful—too beautiful. The temperature was in the high forties at the finish line, and the fat, white clouds had an uncanny knack for dodging the sun. I knew the course would be slower on the second run, the rocks would be sprouting like spring flowers, and I had to be the last one down.

As I waited at the top, again I got alone to recall the Bible verses I had memorized. I tried to visualize the words in my mind. *Whatsoever ye do, do it heartily, as unto the Lord.* I told myself I was committed to Rossignol—I had to do my best. "I don't have any choice. I have to go all out."

All the other racers were now at the bottom of the mountain. I was the only one left, and everyone was waiting to see if I could beat the rocks and hold on for the win.

I put all thoughts of rocks, edges, and falling out of my mind. I skied with total abandon. Nothing was held back. The only thing I thought about was going as fast as possible. I didn't try to avoid the rocks; I blasted right over them.

On the final pitch, suddenly I felt something dragging on my right ski. I could feel it slowing me down, *I've got to get that ski off the snow*, I thought. So I finished the race with all my weight on my left ski, and with only the tail of my right ski brushing the snow. The television commentators kept saying afterwards that it looked like I was about to fall on that last pitch, but I was only trying to keep the ski off the snow. I learned later that a rock had scratched the base of my ski, and the area all around the scratch swelled up to cause the drag.

I shot through the finish and again had to leap off the embankment. Just like the first run, Tommy Waltner came storming after me.

"Way to go! You did it. You beat everybody by a second and a half," he shouted.

I'd done it. For the first time in my life, I'd won a race in international competition.

When the NBC television commentators asked me about the race, I told them I had two secrets.

"First was that I gave away my good racing suit. I thought that would work against me, but apparently it didn't. The second thing is that I've been memorizing Scripture verses with my pastor in Canada as I've trained. Repeating those Bible verses helped me relax and concentrate and ski with abandon. And that's what it takes to win races."

Throughout the rest of my rookie year, I continued to ski better than I'd ever skied before. I won two downhills and wound up finishing third in the WPS standings behind rookie superstar Andre Arnold of Austria and the smooth, sure Swiss, Josef Odermatt. Even greater satisfaction than what came from finally racing the way I knew I could, however, came from the understanding I gained about God and competition.

Always before, I'd felt that God's love was conditional—if I didn't win, he would be displeased. This distorted attitude added so much pressure that I did anything to win, becoming arrogant, self-centered, and obnoxious—anything that I thought would help my skiing. But during the pro season, thanks mostly to the Scripture memorization, I began internalizing the fact that God's perfect peace is a gift. It can't be earned by skiing victories or self-righteous strutting. It only comes when I admit my inadequacy, my sin, and my need, and ask God to forgive me.

It's a lesson I should have learned long ago but didn't. God doesn't necessarily ask us to be successful—he asks us to be faithful. He doesn't use winners all the time; he uses people who say, "Here I am, Lord. I'm available." Knowing that God accepts us in spite of our failures, we don't need to hide them or fear them.

There are nuances of this that I'm still discovering. Sometimes my desire to win, and my disappointment when I don't, still get out of hand. But at last, after ten years of racing, I've finally seen that my winning isn't as important to God as letting

Jim flashes past a giant slalom gate (above) during the 1978 pro races at Winter Park, Colorado. The top three finishers that day (below) were also one-two-three for the season—Andre Arnold (c), Josef Odermatt (l), and Jim Hunter (r).

other people see the love of God in my life.

Sensing that slow, sometimes almost imperceptible change in my personality over the year was the most profound victory of my life.

At the end of the season, Spencer Butts, a pro racer who had known me while I was on the national team, walked up to me to say farewell for the summer.

"I don't believe it," he said. "I've watched you all season, and you've kept your head all year long. You really lived your beliefs. I want you to know it's made a big difference in me and my outlook on life. It's hard for me to believe that you stand up for your faith and take all the stuff you do without blowing up or giving in."

I felt almost as much satisfaction from that observation as I did about placing third. My temperament had always been another huge mountain joined to my desire to win. Thanks to Gail, Bob Cleveland, and God, I was finally beginning to see progress over that mountain of impatience, short temper, and arrogance. I haven't conquered the peak, by any means, but I've made visible progress. One incident in particular encouraged me that I wasn't the same person I had been a year earlier.

In May, I was invited to speak in Toronto at two prayer breakfasts in preparation for the Billy Graham Crusade the next month. Because of schedule problems, one of the breakfasts had to be moved to Friday night at 7 P.M. So I made reservations for an Air Canada plane leaving at 8:30 that morning.

Since I didn't have any luggage except an overnight bag, I got to the check-in counter at 8:22. About six people were lined up at the gate, obviously not very happy, and the girl behind the counter was trying to stay calm.

"Listen," she said. "You were all late, so I gave your seats to the standby passengers. You can't get on the plane."

"Excuse me," I said. "I've got to get to Toronto tonight. I'm supposed to speak at . . ."

"Sorry, you're late. You weren't here ten minutes before departure time. Your reservations were cancelled. You'll have to catch another plane."

While the other would-be passengers got surly, two different voices seemed to start shouting within me. I was detached, listening to them argue.

Well, this is interesting, the first one said. *I guess I'll have to find another plane.*

Why? asked the second voice.

Because I can't go on this one.

Yeah, but you've got to argue at least a little bit.

No, I don't think there's any point in that. She's already made up her mind.

Aw, c'mon. You've got to yell at her—get her uptight. There's an injustice here. You're supposed to be on this flight. You've caught planes at the last minute lots of times. The ticket says you only have to be there five minutes before departure time—not ten minutes like the woman claimed.

No, it's not worth arguing about. Let's find another plane.

I found myself picking up my bag and walking

back down the concourse. Just a year ago, I would have been in the thick of an argument. Now I was looking for another flight.

What am I giving up so easy for? I asked myself. *This isn't me.*

Nevertheless, I went back to the Air Canada ticket counter. The news wasn't good. The noon flight was booked solid, and the next flight wouldn't arrive in Toronto until seven o'clock, the time the meeting started.

I said nothing, but walked over the the CP Air counter. *Scotty Henderson and the guys on the national team wouldn't recognize me,* I thought. I could barely believe it myself.

At CP Air, all the flights to Toronto were full. The only flight I could squeeze onto was one to Winnipeg, but the agent said all the flights from Winnipeg to Toronto were booked solid.

"That's all right. I'll take it."

I figured if God wanted me to get to Toronto on time, he'd make the connections. It was a whole new kind of faith I was exercising. Always before I'd been God's worrier.

As I walked out to board the CP Air flight, I noticed the Air Canada flight that I'd missed pulling back into the gate. Air Canada paged the six people who had been in front of me. Apparently they were bumping the standbys and putting the people with reservations back on. But when I asked about it, the girl said, "I'm sorry, Mr. Hunter, we still don't have a seat for you."

Relax, a voice within said. *Stay cool.*

"Okay," I said, and kept walking to CP Air.

When we arrived at Winnipeg, I grabbed my overnight bag and rushed off the plane to sign up as a standby, hoping that by some long shot, a spot would be open. Several people were standing around the check-in counter, but when I handed my ticket to the girl, she routinely handed me the boarding pass.

"Go right on board, Mr. Hunter."

I was the last person aboard before they shut the door. Settling into my seat, I breathed a sigh of relief and gratitude. It looked like leaving the worrying to God wasn't a bad policy—he seemed to be able to handle it.

Then an intriguing thought struck me—*I wonder why I wasn't supposed to be on that Air Canada flight.* I had a strange hunch that I was learning a valuable lesson here: even when things seem totally out of control, God isn't flustered. He's still in control.

When we landed in Toronto that afternoon, I called Air Canada.

"What time did Flight 110 from Calgary arrive this afternoon?"

"It hasn't arrived yet. Due to mechanical problems before departure, it isn't due to arrive until 7:17 P.M."

With a big grin, I said, "That's the best news I've heard all day."